SURVIVAL JAPANESE

How to communicate without fuss or fear INSTANTLY!

by **BOYÉ LAFAYETTE DE MENTE**
revised edition with Junji Kawai

TUTTLE Publishing

Tokyo │Rutland, Vermont│ Singapore

ABOUT TUTTLE
"Books to Span the East and West"

Our core mission at Tuttle Publishing is to create books which bring people together one page at a time. Tuttle was founded in 1832 in the small New England town of Rutland, Vermont (USA). Our fundamental values remain as strong today as they were then—to publish best-in-class books informing the English-speaking world about the countries and peoples of Asia. The world has become a smaller place today and Asia's economic, cultural and political influence has expanded, yet the need for meaningful dialogue and information about this diverse region has never been greater. Since 1948, Tuttle has been a leader in publishing books on the cultures, arts, cuisines, languages and literatures of Asia. Our authors and photographers have won numerous awards and Tuttle has published thousands of books on subjects ranging from martial arts to paper crafts. We welcome you to explore the wealth of information available on Asia at www.tuttlepublishing.com.

Published by Tuttle Publishing, an imprint of Periplus Editions (HK) Ltd.

www.tuttlepublishing.com

Copyright © 1991 Boyé Lafayette De Mente
Copyright © 2004, 2016 Periplus Editions (HK) Ltd

LCC Card No.: 2009291154
ISBN 978-4-8053-1362-6

20 19 18 17 16   5 4 3 2 1   1510CP
Printed in Singapore

Distributed by:

Japan
Tuttle Publishing
Yaekari Building, 3rd Floor, 5-4-12 Osaki,
Shinagawa-ku, Tokyo 141 0032
Tel: (81) 3 5437-0171; Fax: (81) 3 5437-0755
sales@tuttle.co.jp
www.tuttle.co.jp

North America, Latin America & Europe
Tuttle Publishing
364 Innovation Drive
North Clarendon, VT 05759-9436 U.S.A.
Tel: 1 (802) 773-8930; Fax: 1 (802) 773-6993
info@tuttlepublishing.com
www.tuttlepublishing.com

Asia Pacific
Berkeley Books Pte. Ltd.
61 Tai Seng Avenue #02-12
Singapore 534167
Tel: (65) 6280-1330; Fax: (65) 6280-6290
inquiries@periplus.com.sg
www.periplus.com

CONTENTS

PART 2
Places

PART 3
General Word List

INTRODUCTION

Overcoming Instant Illiteracy

Hundreds of thousands of people who arrive in Japan each year go through an experience that is the equivalent of suddenly being struck deaf and dumb. They go from being literate—even brilliant—in their own culture to not being able to speak, understand, read, or write the language of their host country, and to being equally ignorant of the nonverbal language of Japan as well.

If this situation continues for any length of time, the experience results in a trauma known as culture shock—which in extreme cases can cause serious mental and physical damage; sometimes even death.

Short-time visitors to Japan are not likely to suffer significant health problems because of their sudden inability to interact with the culture surrounding them. But there is perhaps no more frustrating feeling than not being able to communicate with other people when we want to or need to. Where visiting businesspeople are concerned, the handicap of not being able to communicate directly with their Japanese counterparts, even on the most basic level, has far more serious implications.

At a recent dinner in Tokyo with the president of an American company and his Japanese guests, the frustration of the foreign visitor was evident for all to see. Finally, he said in utter exasperation: "God! If I only knew survival Japanese!" That is what this book is all about.

Most people use fewer than 1,000 words of their own native language in going about their daily affairs. It is not so much how many words one knows but what those words are and how they are used. This is particularly true in the case of a second, foreign language. With a vocabulary of only 300 Japanese words you can communicate several thousand ideas—not only enough to survive but also to enjoy yourself at the same time.

Many Americans in particular seem to have a foreign language phobia. Some have extreme difficulty in pronouncing a single foreign word correctly. This fear might be the result of cultural conditioning stemming from a deep-rooted feeling that speaking a foreign language is un-American; that it is a black mark that cannot be erased.

Most Americans are now intellectually sophisticated enough to know this fear of foreign languages is invalid, and to recognize the social as well as economic benefits of being multi-lingual and multi-cultural. But they are still handicapped by the emotional residue of generations of trying to get away from any hint of foreignness.

Survival Japanese provides you with words, phrases and expressions commonly used in the modern Japanese society, both in Romanized Japanese and in Japanese characters, together with a thorough note on pronunciation. I hope this book helps you suppress the emotional reaction to the language and make the first step to communication with the Japanese in Japanese.

How to Use This Book

Despite the forbidding appearance of Japanese when it is written in the Chinese ideograms known as Kanji or "Chinese characters," the language is made up of precise syllables that are in fact quite easy to pronounce (people who are not familiar with the language confuse the difficulty of getting several words out in a smooth flow with a phonetic complexity that does not exist).

Unlike Chinese, Japanese is pronounced in a straightforward manner without complicating tones. The only variations in Japanese are double consonants and long vowels that require a slight change in pronunciation. The grammatical structure of Japanese differs from Chinese as well as English, but that does not make it more difficult to learn. Looking at the order of the subject, verb, and object in a Japanese sentence, saying it is "backward" and complaining that it doesn't make sense is foolish. Of course it makes sense.

Japanese is a very flexible language. You can switch the order of words and phrases around to a surprising degree, even leave things out and it not only makes sense but is acceptable in ordinary conversation. This can be a problem to those who want everything to follow one precise rule and regard this characteristic of the language as a serious complication. But looked at another way, it makes the language easier to use.

There are three distinct levels of Japanese that might be called honorofic, formal and infomal. These levels are different enough that they are practically dialects within themselves. It may be very difficult to become fluent in each of these levels because it is almost like learning separate vocabularies. But being able to communicate effectively in formal Japanese is enough for the average foreigner to at least build a footbridge across the language gap.

Survival Japanese is standard Japanese. I make only a few references to grammar. In the early stages of any language study it often serves only to complicate things. The secret to language learning is to mimic the way native speakers use it, without any thought of its structure. After a while the grammar becomes imprinted on your mind, and making up correctly structured sentences becomes automatic.

This learning process is based on nothing more mysterious than repeating the words and sentences *out loud*, always out loud—a process that imprints the sound on the ear and memory, and just as important if not more so, trains the mouth and tongue to mechanically produce the necessary syllables in a smooth flow.

One of the prime reasons why so many students fail to learn how to speak foreign languages is that they don't speak them enough. You cannot learn a language by looking at it. The whole Japanese language is based on six key sounds which are the building blocks of two sets of syllables. These syllables never change, so once you learn how to pronounce them, you can pronounce any word in the Japanese language. These six sounds and their pronunciations, as written in Roman letters with **hiragana** characters in the brackets, are *a* (あ), *i* (い), *u* (う), *e* (え), *o* (お), and *n* (ん), which is a moraic nasal whose sound is determined by the sound that follows it.

Notes on Pronunciation

Japanese uses *haku* "beat" or more technically, mora, rather than the syllable, as a unit of sounds. *Haku* and syllable are two different units; a Japanese syllable may contain the second half of a long vowel (e.g. *kī*), a moraic nasal (e.g. *ki̲n̲*) or the first half of a double consonant (e.g. *ki̲t.to*), in which case there are two *haku* or two beats within the syllable. So from now on, let's replace the word "syllable" with *haku* or "beat."

There are 101 basic one-*haku* or one-beat sounds called "moraic sounds," which make up the Japanese language. The following table shows those moraic sounds with **hiragana** and **katakana** characters written underneath each of them.

Vowels

a   Similar to the first phase of the diphthong *i* [ai] in "bite." Do not use *a* [ah] in "Bart" or *a* [á] in "bat."

i   Similar to but slightly shorter than *ea* [ii] in "beat." Do not use *i* [í] in "bit."

u   Similar to *oo* [uu] in "boot," but the Japanese *u* is pronounced without rounding the lips.

e   Similar to *e* [é] in "bet."

o   Similar to the first phase of the diphthong *oa* [ou] in "boat" in American English. Do not use *oa* [oo] in "board."

In standard Japanese, the *i* and the *u* are silent or, more technically, voiceless in some words. So, for example, *desu* (です), which is equivalent to "to be," may sound like *dess* and its past tense *deshita* (でした) like *deshta*. However, it is not that the Japanese leave out these vowels; in fact they can still hear the difference between such pairs as *aki* (あき) "fall/autumn" and *aku* (あく) "evil." Therefore, it is best that you always pronounce the *i* and the *u* clearly until you are certain when they become voiceless.

	A	**I**	**U**	**E**	**O**	**YA**	**YU**	**YO**
Vowels	a あ ア	i い イ	u う ウ	e え エ	o お オ			
K	ka か カ	ki き キ	ku く ク	ke け ケ	ko こ コ	kya きゃキャ	kyu きゅキュ	kyo きょキョ
S	sa さ サ	shi し シ	su す ス	se せ セ	so そ ソ	sha しゃシャ	shu しゅシュ	sho しょショ
T	ta た タ	chi ち チ	tsu つ ツ	te て テ	to と ト	cha ちゃチャ	chu ちゅチュ	cho ちょチョ
N	na な ナ	ni に ニ	nu ぬ ヌ	ne ね ネ	no の ノ	nya にゃニャ	nyu にゅニュ	nyo にょニョ
H	ha は ハ	hi ひ ヒ	fu ふ フ	he へ ヘ	ho ほ ホ	hya ひゃヒャ	hyu ひゅヒュ	hyo ひょヒョ
M	ma ま マ	mi み ミ	mu む ム	me め メ	mo も モ	mya みゃミャ	myu みゅミュ	myo みょミョ
Y	ya や ヤ		yu ゆ ユ		yo よ ヨ			
R	ra ら ラ	ri り リ	ru る ル	re れ レ	ro ろ ロ	rya りゃリャ	ryu りゅリュ	ryo りょリョ
W	wa わ ワ				(o) を ヲ			
Moraic Nasal	n ん ン							

Long vowels

In Japanese, short vowels (e.g. *i*) and long vowels (e.g. *ii*) are used contrastively to differentiate the meaning of words. For example, *ojisan* (おじさん) means "uncle" while *ojiisan* (おじいさん) means "grandfather." Long vowels are more or less twice as long as short vowels, and it is important to learn to pronounce vowels with the right length.

A long vowel may be indicated in Romanized Japanese by a line above the letter. In *Survival Japanese*, however, a phonetic second letter is added after the vowel as a pronunciation aid, as *ā*, *ī*, *ū*, *ē* and *ō*.

G	ga が ガ	gi ぎ ギ	gu ぐ グ	ge げ ゲ	go ご ゴ	gya ぎゃギャ	gyu ぎゅギュ	gyo ぎょギョ
Z	za ざ ザ	zi じ ジ	zu ず ズ	ze ぜ ゼ	zo ぞ ゾ	ja じゃジャ	ju じゅジュ	jo じょジョ
D(J)	da だ ダ	(ji) ぢ ヂ	(zu) づ ヅ	de で デ	do ど ド	(ja) ぢゃヂャ	(ju) ぢゅヂュ	(jo) ぢょヂョ
P	pa ぱ パ	pi ぴ ピ	pu ぷ プ	pe ぺ ペ	po ぽ ポ	pya ぴゃピャ	pyu ぴゅピュ	pyo ぴょピョ
B	ba ば バ	bi び ビ	bu ぶ ブ	be べ ベ	bo ぼ ボ	bya びゃビャ	byu びゅビュ	byo びょビョ

Moraic nasal

'n' is a moraic nasal, which requires the same length of time as all the other moraic sounds. How it is pronounced depends on what sound follows it. It is pronounced as:

- *n* when followed by *t*, *d*, *z*, *r* or *n* (e.g. *hontō* ほんとう);
- *m* when followed by *p*, *b* or *m* (e.g. *tenpura* てんぷら). (In English the prefix *in* is replaced with *im* before these consonants but in Japanese *n* is still used to represent *m*.);
- *ng* as in "singer" when followed by *k* or *g* (e.g. *tenki* てんき);
- a nasalized sound of the preceding vowel when followed by *s*, *h*, *y*, *w* or a vowel (e.g. *kinshi* きんし, *ren'ai* れんあい). (In American English, vowels are normally nasalized when followed by a nasal sound, as in "can" and "internet." In Japanese a nasal is vocalized instead.) For example, *konbanwa* (こんばんは), a five-beat (*ko.n.ba.n.wa*) three-syllable (*kon.ban.wa*) word meaning "good evening," is pronounced as [*kombaãwa*] ([ã] nasalized [a]).

Consonants

The following moraic sounds and consonants require special attention:

tsu   The only English word containing this sequence of sounds is "tsunami," which is a loanword from Japanese. Try pronouncing *tsu* by isolating *ts* from "cats" and adding *u* to it.

hi   The "h" of *hi* is much closer to the German "ch" in "ich" than the English "h" in "he." It has more friction of air than its English counterpart.

fu   "f" is conventionally used to represent this consonant sound, but actually it is not "f" at all. Imagine you are blowing a candle very gently. That is exactly how this sound is produced.

r   It has two sounds depending on where it is used. Between vowels (e.g. **te_ra** てら) it is a flap, which can be heard in such words as "ri_der," "wa_ter," and "bo_ttom" in American English, but at the beginning of a word (e.g. **_roku** ろく) most Japanese people use *l* instead of a flap, and *l* is exclusively used after a moraic nasal *n* (e.g. **ten_ran** てんらん). When it is followed by *y*, a flap is used at the beginning of a word (e.g. **_ryokō** りょこう) but *l* remains the same after a moraic nasal (e.g. **en_ryo** えんりょ).

g   It is always pronounced hard, even before the *i* and the *e*. In standard Japanese, it is often nasalized between vowels (e.g. **kai_gi** かいぎ) as *ng* in "singer."

Double consonants

Some words have a double consonant, *pp*, *tt* (or *tch* before *i* and *tts* before *u*), *kk*, or *ss* (or *ssh*). The first half of the double consonant, which is transcribed with っ, belongs to the preceding syllable and the second half forms a syllable

with the vowel. The first half is a kind of preparation time
for the second half and it requires one beat, just like all the
other moraic sounds. No sound is audible while the first half
is pronounced, except in the case of *ss* where a hissing sound
can be heard.

e.g. *ki·p·pu*   (きっぷ)   ticket
　　　 1 2 3
　　 ki·t·te   (きって)   stamp
　　 1 2 3
　　 za·s·shi   (ざっし)   magazine
　　 1 2 3

There are pairs of words and phrases, one with a single con-
sonant and the other with a double consonant, such as *kite ku-dasai* (きてください) "please come" and *kitte kudasai* (きってくだ
さい) "please cut." It is absolutely necessary to "hit" a double
consonant clearly to be understood.

Other moraic sounds

The following table shows the rest of the moraic sounds,
which are exclusively used to transcribe loanwords (note that
loanwords are conventionally written in **katakana**):

	A	I	U	E	O
F	fa ファ	fi フィ	fu フ	fe フェ	fo フォ
V	va ヴァ	vi ヴィ	vu ヴ	ve ヴェ	vo ヴォ
W		wi ウィ		we ウェ	wo ウォ
T		ti ティ	tu トゥ		
D		di ディ	du ドゥ		

e.g.
forudā
(フォルダー)
folder
webusaito
(ウェブサイト)
website
shīdī
(シーディー)
CD

Accent

Japanese is a pitch accent language, as opposed to English being a stress accent language. This means that accentuation is made with the pitch of the voice and that to this end either a high or low pitch is assigned to each **haku** or beat of a word. For example, **tōkyō** (とうきょう) "Tokyo," **nihon** (にほん) "Japan," and **kyōto** (きょうと) "Kyoto" are pronounced as follows (H: high pitch, L: low pitch):

to o kyo o	ni ho n	kyo o to
L H H H	L H L	H L L

The pitch is often used to differentiate the meaning of homophones, such as **hashi** (はし:HL) "chopsticks" and **hashi** (はし: LH) "bridge." Therefore, if you are really serious about mastering the language, it is highly recommended that you purchase a dictionary that shows the accent of each word and remember it together with the word.

However, even if you pronounce words with the incorrect accent, the Japanese should be able to understand you when you use them in the correct context. For this reason, and in order to reduce the burden of your learning, no accent mark is added to words in this book.

Dealing with Grammar

Word order
The grammatical order of Japanese is subject-object-verb, instead of the subject-verb-object form of English. Having said that, I suggest that you ignore it for the time being (although this is probably the reason why the subject is often left out in Japanese conversation when the meaning is clear without it, and why the verb is often used by itself, playing the role of all the parts of speech).

The verb "to be"
The all important "I am; he/she is; we/you/they are" are all expressed in Japanese by *desu* (です). The past tense of *desu* (です), expressing "I/he/she was; we/you/they were," is *deshita* (でした).

"There is/are"
There are several ways to express "there is" and "there are." When referring to human beings, use

orimasu (おります) for yourself or your family/in-group members when you need to be humble.

imasu (います) for anyone, you, your friends, etc. when you do not need to be humble.

irasshaimasu (いらっしゃいます) for someone you should pay respect to.

When referring to animals, *imasu* (います) is also used. When referring to inanimate objects, *arimasu* (あります) is used. For the past tense of these words, simply replace *masu* (ます) with *mashita* (ました).

Singular/plural

There is no definite or indefinite article (i.e. the, a) in Japanese, and there are very few plurals in the language. With few exceptions, the sense of plural is made evident by the context of the phrase or sentence. *Tokei* (とけい) means watch (timepiece) or watches, depending on how it is used.

Superlative

It is very easy to "make" the superlative in Japanese. All you do is put the word *ichiban* (いちばん), meaning "first" or "number one" in front of the term you want to qualify. If big is *ōkii* (おおきい), the biggest is *ichiban ōkii* (いちばんおおきい); the longest is *ichiban nagai* (いちばんながい); the smallest is *ichiban chiisai* (いちばんちいさい); the highest is *ichiban takai* (いちばんたかい); the heaviest is *ichiban omoi* (いちばんおもい); the best is *ichiban ii* (いちばんいい), and so on.

Questions

In Japanese a question is indicated by the particle *ka* (か), usually enunciated with the same "questioning" tone used in English. In written Japanese this *ka* (か) takes the place of the familiar question mark.

The honorific "O"

It is customary in Japanese to add an honorific "o" or "go" before many words that refer to other people, to things relating to others, and to certain special words, as a sign of respect or as a polite gesture. In the sign-of-respect category are such words as *go-shujin* (ごしゅじん), meaning "your honorable" husband; *o-taku* (おたく), "your honorable" residence; *o-namae* (おなまえ), "your honorable" name; *o-toshi* (おとし), "your honorable" age, and *o-denwa-bangō* (おでんわばんご

う), "your honorable" phone number. In the polite category are such words as weather (*o-tenki* おてんき), sake or rice wine (*o-sake* おさけ), money (*o-kane* おかね), boxed lunch (*o-bentō* おべんとう), chopsticks (*o-hashi* おはし), bath (*o-furo* おふろ), temple (*o-tera* おてら), and New Year's (*o-shōgatsu* おしょうがつ). In many cases, these "o" and "go" honorifics have more or less become a part of the words they precede and are generally included regardless of the circumstances.

PART ONE
Common Expressions & Key Words

KEYS WORDS

I   *watashi (wah-tah-she)* わたし—Used by both males and females in formal situations.

   watakushi (wah-tock-she) わたくし—More formal than *watashi*.

   boku (boe-kuu) ぼく—Used by boys and men in informal situations.

   ore (oh-ray) おれ—A 'rough' term used by males in informal situations.

   washi (wah-she) わし—Sometimes used by elderly men in informal situations.

   atashi (ah-tah-she) あたし—Mainly used by girls and women in informal situations.

   NOTE : When talking about oneself, these terms are normally followed by *wa* (は topic marker), as in *watashi-wa amerika-jin-desu (wah-tah-she wah ah-may-ree-kah-jeen dess)* わたしはアメリカじんです "I am American."

me   Any of the above terms used in the objective sense, in which case they are usually used with *o (oh)* (を direct object marker) or *ni (nee)* (に indirect object marker). For example,

   watashi-o shōkai-shimashita (wah-tah-she oh show-kie she-mah-sshtah) わたしを　しょうかいしました

"(Someone) introduced me (to someone else)."
watashi-ni shōkai-shimashita (*wah-tah-she nee show-kie she-mah-sshtah*) わたしに　しょうかいしました "(Someone) introduced (someone else) to me."

my   Any of the above "I" words followed by **no** *(no)* (の possessive marker). "My book," for example, is ***watashi-no hon*** (*wah-tah-she no hoan*) わたしの ほん, ***boku-no hon*** (*boe-kuu no hoan*) ぼくの　ほん, and so forth.

mine   Any of the above "I" words with **no** *(no)* の alone, i.e. ***watashi-no*** (*wah-tah-she-no*) わたしの, ***boku-no*** (*boe-kuu no*) ぼくの, and so forth.

we   The "we" concept is formed by adding ***tachi*** (*tah-chee*) たち to any of the above forms of "I," i.e.: ***watashi-tachi*** (*wah-tah-she-tah-chee*) わたしたち, ***boku-tachi*** (*boe-kuu-tah-chee*) ぼくたち, and so forth.

you   ***anata*** (*ah-nah-tah*) あなた—Used by both males and females when addressing a stranger, or by women when addressing their husbands. In the latter case, ***anata*** is the equivalent of "dear."
kimi (*kee-me*) きみ—Used by males when addressing females in informal situations.
anta (*ahn-tah*) あんた—Used by both males and females in informal situations.
omae (*o-mah-eh*) おまえ—A 'rough' term used by males in informal situations.

NOTE: The plural of "you" is formed by adding the suffix *gata (gah-tah)* がた, which is polite, or *tachi (tah-chee)* たち, which is less formal: ***anata-gata*** *(ah-nah-tah-gah-tah)* あなたがた, ***anata-tachi*** *(ah-nah-tah-tah-chee)* あなたたち.

In Japanese, "you" is hardly ever used unless the speaker doesn't know the listener's name. Otherwise, his/her name is used to address the listener, as in ***kore-wa tomu-san-no-desu-ka*** *(koe-ray wah toe-moo-sahn no dess kah)* これはトムさんのですか "Is this yours, Tom?"

he   ***ano hito*** *(ah-no-he-toe)* あのひと, or more polite, ***ano kata*** *(ah-no-kah-tah)* あのかた, both of which literally mean "that person."
kare *(kah-ray)* かれ—Sometimes used by both males and females in informal situations. It can also mean "boyfriend."

she   ***ano hito*** *(ah-no-he-toe)* あのひと, or more polite, ***ano kata*** *(ah-no-kah-tah)* あのかた.
kanojo *(kah-no-joe)* かのじょ—Sometimes used by both males and females in informal situations. It can also mean "girlfriend."

they   ***ano kata-gata*** *(ah-no-kah-tah-gah-tah)* あのかたがた, which is polite, or ***ano hito-tachi*** *(ah-no-he-toe-tah-chee)* あのひとたち, which is less polite.

In conversation, "he," "she" and "they" are frequently not used. The practice is to use the name of the individual concerned in order to be more specific and personal. It is also common practice to leave out "I" and "you" when the meaning is clear from the context, often subsuming the meaning in the verb form used. For example, "are you going?" is often just expressed as ***ikimasu-ka*** *(ee-kee-mahss kah)* いきますか, which technically means "going?" with the "you" understood. The usual answer would be ***ikimasu*** *(ee-kee-mahss)* いきます "going," meaning, of course, "I am going."

who   ***donata*** *(doe-nah-tah)* どなた, or less formal, ***dare*** *(dah-ray)* だれ.
When used as the subject, the "who" words are followed by ***ga*** *(gah)* (が subject marker), as in ***dare-ga ikimasu-ka*** *(dah-ray-gah ee-kee-mahss kah)* だれが いきますか "Who is going?"

what   ***nani*** *(nah-nee)* なに often shortened to ***nan*** *(nahn)* なん before certain sounds.

when   ***itsu*** *(eet-sue)* いつ

where ***doko*** *(doe-koe)* どこ

why   ***naze*** *(nah-zay)* なぜ, also ***dōshite*** *(doe-ssh-tay)* どうして

how   ***dō*** *(doh)* どう

yes   ***hai*** *(hie)* はい, also ***ee*** *(eh-eh)* ええ, which is less formal.

Hai (or *ee*) is quite often used in the sense of "yes, I hear you" or "yes, I'm listening" in conversation, particularly when talking on the phone. Bear in mind that this use of ***hai*** (or ***ee***) does not mean "you are right" or "I agree with you."

no   *iie (ee-eh)* いいえ , also *ie (e-eh)* いえ,
             which is less formal.

Iie (or ie) is used more often to mean "no" than *hai (or ee)*
is to mean "yes." However, Japanese do not like to say "no"
outright unless the situation is informal or they are answering
a simple yes-no question, such as "Do you know Mr. Smith?"
Especially in business they usually couch the concept in more
subtle forms and try to avoid saying "no."

Here are some commonly used verbs, presented first in the
dictionary form (i.e. the plain non-past affirmative form,
which you can find in a dictionary), then in the stem form, the
*te-*form (a sort of present participle), and the *nai-*form (i.e.
the plain non-past negative form). There are two tenses in
Japanese, namely, the non-past tense, which corresponds to
the English present and future tenses, and the past tense. The
following table shows how to conjugate verbs:

	Affirmative forms	Negative forms
Polite non-past forms	Stem form + *masu* (ます)	Stem form + *masen* (ません)
Polite past forms	Stem form + *mashita* (ました)	Stem form + *masendeshita* (ませんでした)
Polite desiderative forms	Stem form + *tai-desu* (たいです)	Stem form + *takunai-desu* (たくないです)
Polite imperative forms	*Te-*form + *kudasai* (ください)	*Nai-*form + *de kudasai* (でください)

For example,
buy   *kau (kah-uu)* かう, *kai (kie)* かい,
           katte (kot-tay) かって,

kawanai (kah-wah-nie) かわない,
kaimasu (kie-mahss) かいます "buy / will buy."
kaimasen (kie-mah-sen) かいません
"do not buy / will not buy."
kaimashita (kie-mah-sshtah) かいました "bought."
kaimasendeshita (kie-mah-sen desh-tah)
かいませんでした "did not buy."
kaitai-desu (kie-tie dess) かいたいです "want to buy."
kaitakunai-desu かいたくないです
(kie-tah-kuu-nie dess) "do not want to buy."
katte kudasai かってください
(kot-tay kuu-dah-sie) "please buy."
kawanaide kudasai かわないでください
(kah-wah-nie day kuu-dah-sie) "please do not buy."

Note that the subject (**I**, **you**, **he**, **she**, **we** or **they**) is usually omitted when it is easily understood from the context.

To change them to the interrogative form, simply add *ka* *(kah)* (か question marker) to the end (e.g. *kaimasu-ka (kie-mahss kah)* かいますか "buy?", *kaimashita-ka (kie-mahssh-tah kah)* かいましたか "bought?").

come   *kuru (kuu-rue)* くる, *ki (kee)* き,
            kite (kee-tay) きて, *konai (koe-nie)* こない.

drink   *nomu (no-muu)* のむ, *nomi (no-me)* のみ,
            nonde (noan-day) のんで,
            nomanai (no-mah-nie) のまない.

eat   *taberu (tah-bay-rue)* たべる,
            tabe (tah-bay) たべ,
            tabete (tah-bay-tay) たべて,
            tabenai (tah-bay-nie) たべない.

forget   *wasureru (wah-sue-ray-rue)* わすれる,
      wasure (wah-sue-ray) わすれ,
      wasurete (wah-sue-ray-tay) わすれて,
      wasurenai (wah-sue-ray-nie) わすれない.

give (to someone)
      ageru (ah-gay-rue) あげる,
      age (ah-gay) あげ,
      agete (ah-gay-tay) あげて,
      agenai (ah-gay-nie) あげない.

give (to me)
      kureru (kuu-ray-rue) くれる,
      kure (kuu-ray) くれ,
      kurete (kuu-ray-tay) くれて,
      kurenai (kuu-ray-nie) くれない.

Note that "please give me" is simply *kudasai (kuu-dah-sie)* く
ださい, not *kurete kudasai (kuu-ray-tay kuu-dah-sie)* くれて
ください.

go   *iku (ee-koo)* いく, *iki (ee-kee)* いき,
      itte (eet-tay) いって,
      ikanai (ee-kah-nie) いかない.

hear   *kiku (kee-koo)* きく, *kiki (kee-kee)* きき,
      kiite (kee-tay) きいて,
      kikanai (kee-kah-nie) きかない.

have   *motsu (moe-t'se)* もつ, *mochi (moe-chee)* もち,
      motte (moat-tay) もって,
      motanai (moe-tah-nie) もたない.

Note that, instead of the stem form, ***motte-i*** (もってい *te-*form + *i* い) is used in the non-past and past forms *(e.g.* ***motte-imasu*** *(moat-tay ee-mahss)* もっています "have," ***motte-imasen*** *(moat-tay ee-mah-sen)* もっていません "do not have"*)*.

know   ***shiru*** *(she-rue)* しる, ***shiri*** *(she-ree)* しり, ***shitte*** *(ssh-tay)* しって, ***shiranai*** *(she-rah-nie)* しらない.

Note that in the affirmative forms ***shitte-i*** (しってい *te-*form + *i* い) replaces the stem form, with the exception of the desiderative form *(e.g.* ***shitte-imasu***? *(ssh-tay-ee-mahss)* しっています "know," ***shitte-imashita*** *(ssh-tay-ee-mah-sshtah)* しっていました "knew," but ***shiritaidesu*** *(she-ree-tie-dess)* しりたいです "want to know"*)*.

read   ***yomu*** *(yoe-muu)* よむ, ***yomi*** *(yoe-me)* よみ, ***yonde*** *(yoan-day)* よんで, ***yomanai*** *(yoe-mah-nie)* よまない.

return (go/come back*)*
    kaeru *(kah-eh-rue)* かえる, ***kaeri*** *(kah-eh-ree)* かえり, ***kaette*** *(kah-eh't-tay)* かえって, ***kaeranai*** *(kah-eh-rah-nie)* かえらない.

say   ***iu*** *(yuu)* いう, ***ii*** *(ee)* いい, ***itte*** *(eet-tay)* いって, ***iwanai*** *(e-wah-nie)* いわない.

see (someone)

au (a-uu) あう, *ai (ai)* あい,
atte (at-tay) あって,
awanai (ah-wah-nie) あわない.

see (something)

miru (me-rue) みる, *mi (me)* み,
mite (me-tay) みて, *minai (me-nie)* みない.

sleep

neru (ney-rue) ねる, *ne (ney)* ね,
nete (nay-tay) ねて, *nenai (nay-nie)* ねない.

speak

hanasu (hah-nah-sue) はなす,
hanashi (hah-nah-ssh) はなし,
hanashite (hah-nah-sshtay) はなして,
hanasanai (hah-nah-sah-nie) はなさない.

understand

wakaru (wah-kah-rue) わかる,
wakari (wah-kah-ree) わかり,
wakatte (wah-kot-tay) わかって,
wakaranai (wah-kah-rah-nie) わからない.

walk

aruku (ah-rue-kuu) あるく,
aruki (ah-rue-kee) あるき,
aruite (ah-rue-ee-tay) あるいて,
arukanai (ah-rue-kah-nie) あるかない.

wait

matsu (mah-t'sue) まつ,
machi (mah-chee) まち,
matte (maht-tay) まって,
matanai (mah-tah-nie) またない.

write   *kaku (kah-kuu)* かく, *kaki (kah-kee)* かき,
        kaite (kie-tay) かいて,
        kakanai (kah-kah-nie) かかない.

COMMON PHRASES

▶ **Do you speak English?**
  Eigo-o hanashimasu-ka. えいごを　はなしますか。
  (Aa-go oh hah-nah-she-mahss kah)

Note that the Japanese full stop is a small circle, which is used
whether the sentence is a statement or a question.

▶ **I can speak a little Japanese.**
  Nihongo-ga sukoshi hanasemasu.
  (Nee-hoan-go gah suu-koe-she hah-nah-say-mahss)
  にほんごが　すこし　はなせます。

▶ **I don't understand.**
  Wakarimasen. (Wah-kah-ree-mah-sen) わかりません。

▶ **Please say it again.**
  Mō ichido itte kudasai. もういちど　いって　ください。
  (Moe ee-chee-doe eet-tay kuu-dah-sie)

▶ **Please speak more slowly.**
  Mō sukoshi yukkuri hanashite kudasai.
  (Moe suu-koe-shee yuke-kuu-ree hah-nah-sshtay kuu-dah-sie)
  もうすこし　ゆっくり　はなして　ください。

► **I understand.**
Wakarimashita. *(Wah-kah-ree-mah-sshtah)*
わかりました。

Note the change in the tense.

► **Do you understand?**
Wakarimashita-ka. わかりましたか。
(Wah-kah-ree-mah-sshtah kah)

► **I want to study Japanese.**
Nihongo-o benkyō-shitai-desu.
(Nee-hoan-go oh bane-k'yoe she-tie dess)
にほんごを　べんきょう　したいです。

► **Please speak in Japanese.**
Nihongo-de hanashite kudasai.
(Nee-hoan-go day hah-nah-sshtay kuu-dah-sie)
にほんごで　はなして　ください。

► **Is it all right?**
Ii-desu-ka. *(ee-dess-kah)* いいですか。

► **It's OK.**
Daijōbu-desu. *(Die-joe-buu dess)* だいじょうぶです。

► **Please.**
Onegai-shimasu. おねがいします。
(Oh-nay-guy-she-mahss)

► **It doesn't matter. / I don't mind.**
Kamaimasen. *(Kah-my-mah-sen)* かまいません。

▶ **I see. / Is that so?**
Sō-desu-ka. (Soh dess kah) そうですか。

▶ **I don't want/need it.**
Irimasen. (Ee-ree-mah-sen) いりません。/
Kekkō-desu. (more polite) けっこうです。
(Keck-koe dess)

▶ **I think so.**
Sō omoimasu. そう　おもいます。
(Soh oh-moy-ee-mahss)

▶ **I don't think so.**
Sō-wa omoimasen. そうは　おもいません。
(Soh wah oh-moy-mah-sen)
Chigau-to omoimasu. ちがうと　おもいます。
(Chee-gah-uu toe oh-moy-ee-mahss)

▶ **Not yet.** (Used as a sentence.)
Mada-desu. (Mah-dah dess) まだです。

▶ **Just a moment, please.**
Chotto matte kudasai. ちょっと　まって　ください。
(Choat-toe mot-tay kuu-dah-sie)

Chotto (choat-toe) ちょっと is also used by itself when you
want to get someone's attention and/or call the person to
you—*Chotto! (choat-toe)* ちょっと . This is very familiar,
however, and is primarily used among families and when
addressing serving people in an informal setting, such as a
restaurant. When said in a reluctant, cautious tone of voice,
chotto means you don't want to positively respond to a ques-

tion or comment, and are leaving it to the listener to interpret your meaning. If someone says *chotto muzukashii-desu-ne* (*choat-toe muu-zuu-kah-she dess nay*) ちょっと　むずかし いですね。"it's a little difficult," they really mean it can't be done or they can't do it.

▶ **I've had enough / No more, thank you.**
   Mō kekkō-desu. もうけっこうです。
   (*Moe keck-koe dess*)

▶ **Well, I must be going.**
   Jā soro-soro shitsurei-shimasu.
   (*Jah so-roe so-roe she-t'sue-ray she-mahss*)
   じゃあ　そろそろ　しつれいします。

▶ **Where did you study English?**
   Doko-de Eigo-o benkyō-shimashita-ka.
   (*Doe-koe day aa-go oh bane-k'yoe she-mah-sshta kah*)
   どこで　えいごを　べんきょう　しましたか。

▶ **Have you been to the United States?**
   Amerika-ni itta koto-ga arimasu-ka.
   (*Ah-may-ree-kah nee eet-tah koe-toe gah ah-ree-mahss kah*)
   アメリカに　いったことが　ありますか。

GREETING PEOPLE

Good morning. (Said until about 11:00 a.m.)
Ohayō gozaimasu. おはよう　ございます。
(*Oh-hah-yoe go-zie-mahss*)

Good afternoon.
(Said from around 11:00 a.m. until dusk.)
Konnichiwa. (Kone-nee-chee wah) こんにちは。

Note that *konnichiwa* is not used among family members or close friends, or between colleagues in their workplace.

Good evening. (Said from dusk.)
Konbanwa. (Kome-bahn wah) こんばんは。

Note that *konbanwa* is not used among family members or close friends, or between colleagues in their workplace.

Good night.
Oyasumi-nasai. おやすみなさい。
(Oh-yah-sue-me nah-sie)

▶ **See you again tomorrow.**
  Mata ashita. (Mah-tah ah-ssh-tah) また　あした。

▶ **How are you?**
  O-genki-desu-ka. おげんきですか。
  (Oh-gain-kee dess kah)

Note that Japanese do not say this to people they meet regularly or to strangers.

▶ **I'm fine.**
  Genki-desu. (Gain-kee dess) げんきです。

▶ **I'm fine, thanks to you.** (A set expression.)
  Ee, okagesama-de. ええ、おかげさまで。
  (Feh-eh oh-kah-gay-sah-mah day)

This phrase is used in reply to *o-genki-desu-ka* *(oh-gain-kee dess kah)* It literally means "yes, thanks to you."

► **It's been a long time, hasn't it!**
  O-hisashiburi-desu-ne. おひさしぶりですね。
  (Oh-he-sah-she-buu-ree dess nay)
  Shibaraku-desu-ne. しばらくですね。
  (Shee-bah-rah-kuu dess nay)

► **I've been out of touch for a long time!**
  Gobusata-shite-imashita. ごぶさたして　いました。
  (Go-buu-sah-tah she-tay ee-mah-sshtah)

This phrase is often used when meeting someone after having been out of touch for a long time and you feel a bit guilty.

FAMILY TERMS

► **How is your wife?**
  Oku-san-wa ikaga-desu-ka.
  (Oak-sahn wah ee-kah-gah dess kah)
  おくさんは　いかがですか。

► **How is your husband?**
  Go-shujin-wa ikaga-desu-ka.
  (Go-shuu-jean wah ee-kah-gah dess kah)
  ごしゅじんは　いかがですか。

► **She/He is well, thank you.**
  Okagesama-de genki-desu. おかげさまで　げんきです。
  (Oh-kah-gay-sah-mah day, gain-kee dess)

	Your/Someone else...	My ...
Wife	*Oku-san* (Oak-sahn) おくさん	*Kanai* (Kah-nie) かない
Husband	*Go-shujin* (Go-shuu-jean) ごしゅじん	*Shujin* (Shuu-jean) しゅじん
Child/children	*O-ko-san* (Oh-koe-sahn) おこさん	*Kodomo* (Koe-doe-moe) おこさん
Daughter(s)	*O-jō-san* (Oh-joe-sahn) おじょうさん	*Musume* (Muu-sue-may) むすめ
Son(s)	*Musuko-san* (Muu-sue-koe-sahn) むすこさん	*Musuko* (Muu-sue-koe) むすこ

▶ **How do you feel?**

(Said to someone who has been ill.)

Go-kibun-wa ikaga-desu-ka?

(Go-kee-boon wah ee-kah-gah dess kah)

ごきぶんは　いかがですか。

▶ **I'm better now, thank you.**

Okagesama-de yoku narimashita.

(Oh-kah-gay-sah-mah day yoe-kuu nah-ree-mah-sshtah)

おかげさまで　よく　なりました。

▶ **Welcome.**

Irasshaimase. (Ee-rash-shy-mah-say) いらっしゃいませ。

This is the polite, formal expression commonly used in an institutionalized way when welcoming people to your home, etc. It is also the expression that restaurant/bar staff and shop assistants traditionally call out when customers enter.

INTRODUCTIONS

introduce	*shōkai-suru* しょうかいする *(show-kie-sue-rue)*
letter of introduction	*shōkaijō* しょうかいじょう *(show-kie-joe)*
name	*namae (nah-mah-eh)* なまえ

The similarity in spelling is coincidental.

name-card	*meishi (may-she)* めいし

▶ **Let me introduce myself.**
Jiko-shōkai sasete kudasai.
(Jee-koe show-kie sa-say-tay kuu-dah-sie)
じこしょうかい　させて　ください。

▶ **My name is De Mente.**
Watashi-no namae-wa De Mente-desu.
(Wah-tock-she no nah-mah-eh wah De Mente dess)
わたしの　なまえは　デ・メンテです。
De Mente-to mōshimasu. (more formal)
(De Mente toe moe-ssh-mahss)
デ・メンテと　もうします。

In business this is the time when you present your name-card
to the listener. When giving and receiving a name-card, it is
good manner to hold it with both hands.

▶ **What is your name?**
O-namae-wa nan-desu-ka? おなまえは　なんですか。
(Oh-nah-mah-eh wah nahn dess kah)

▶ **Pardon me for asking your name.** (more polite)
Shitsurei-desu-ga, dochira-sama-deshō-ka.
(She-t'sue-ray dess gah doe-chee-rah sah-mah day-show kah)
しつれいですが、 どちらさまでしょうか。

▶ **Could you introduce me to that person, please?**
Ano kata-ni shōkai-shite kudasaimasen-ka.
(Ah-no-kah-tah nee show-kie she-tay kuu-dah-sie mah-sen kah)
あの かたに しょうかいして くださいませんか。

▶ **This is Mr. Tanaka.**
Kochira-wa Tanaka-san-desu. こちらは たなかさんです。
(Koe-chee-rah wah Tah-nah-kah-sahn dess)

▶ **How do you do?**
Hajimemashite. (Hah-jee-may-mah-ssh-tay) はじめまして。

▶ **I'm pleased to meet you.**
Dōzo yoroshiku onegai-shimasu.
(Doe-zoe yoe-roe-she-kuu oh-nay-guy-she-mahss)
どうぞ よろしく おねがいします。

This phrase is often shortened to *yoroshiku onegai-shimasu*
(yoe-roe-she-kuu oh-nay-guy-she-mahss) よろしく おねがい
します, or to *dōzo yoroshiku (doe-zoe yoe-roe-she-kuu)* どう
ぞ よろしく when the situation is not very formal.

▶ **May I have one of your name-cards?**
O-meishi-o itadakemasen-ka.
(Oh-may-she oh ee-tah-dah-kay mah-sen kah)
おめいしを いただけませんか。

▶ **Please come in.**
Dōzo, o-hairi-kudasai. どうぞ、おはいりください。
(Doe-zoe, oh-hie-ree kuu-dah-sie)

▶ **Please sit down (on a chair).**
Dōzo, o-kake-kudasai. どうぞ、おかけください。
(Doe-zoe, oh-kah-kay kuu-dah-sie)

▶ **Please sit down (on a cushion on the floor).**
Dōzo, o-suwari-kudasai. どうぞ、おすわりください。
(Doe-zoe, oh-sue-wah-ree kuu-dah-sie)

▶ **Thank you very much.**
(Said when entering a room or sitting down.)
Hai, shitsurei-shimasu. はい、 しつれいします。
(Hie, she-t'sue-ray she-mahss)

This expression literally means "yes, excuse me (for entering your room / for sitting down)."

▶ **Thank you very much.** (Said after receiving a favor.)
Arigatō gozaimasu. ありがとう　ございます。
(Ah-ree-gah-toe go-zie-mahss)

▶ **Don't mention it. / You're welcome.**
Dō itashimashite. どういたしまして。
(Doe ee-tah-she-mah-sshtay)

IN A TAXI

left	*hidari (he-dah-ree)* ひだり
right	*migi (me-ghee)* みぎ
straight	*massugu (mahss-sue-guu)* まっすぐ
intersection	*kōsaten (koe-sah-ten)* こうさてん
corner	*kado (kah-doe)* かど
address	*jūsho (juu-show)* じゅうしょ

► **Please go to ...**
  ...-ni itte kudasai. ……に　いってください。
  (... nee eat-tay kuu-dah-sie)
  ...-made onegai-shimasu.
  (... mah-day oh-nay-guy-she-mahss)
  ……まで　おねがいします。

► **I want to go to this address.**
  Kono jūsho-ni ikitai-n-desu-kedo.
  (Koe-no juu-show nee ee-kee-tien dess kay-doe)
  この　じゅうしょに　いきたいんですけど。

► **Please go to Roppongi.**
  Roppongi-ni itte kudasai.
  (Rope-pon-ghee nee eat-tay kuu-dah-sie)
  ろっぽんぎに　いってください。
  Roppongi-made onegai-shimasu.
  (Rope-pon-ghee mah-day oh-nay-guy-she-mahss)
  ろっぽんぎまで　おねがいします。

▶ **Please go to the Hotel New Otani.**
   Hoteru-nyū-ōtani-ni itte kudasai.
   (Hoe-tay-rue ne-yuu-oh-tah-nee-nee eat-tay kuu-dah-sie)
   ホテルニューオータニに　いってください。

▶ **Do you know the Nomura Securities Building?**
   Nomura shōken biru-o shitte-imasu-ka.
   (No-muu-rah show-ken bee-rue oh ssh-tay ee-mahss kah)
   のむらしょうけんビルを　しっていますか。

▶ **How many minutes is it to Shinjuku?**
   Shinjuku-made nanpun-gurai-desu-ka.
   (Sheen-juu-kuu mah-day nahn poon guu-rye dess kah)
   しんじゅくまで　なんぷんぐらいですか。

▶ **Please hurry.**
   Isoide kudasai.
   (Ee-so-ee-day kuu-dah-sie)
   いそいで　ください。

▶ **Please turn left there.**
   Soko-o hidari-ni magatte kudasai.
   (Soe-koe oh he-dah-ree nee mah-got-tay kuu-dah-sie)
   そこを　ひだりに　まがってください。

▶ **Turn right at the next corner.**
   Tsugi-no kado-o migi-ni magatte kudasai.
   (Tsue-ghee no kah-doe oh me-ghee nee mah-got-tay kuu-dah-sie)
   つぎの　かどを　みぎに　まがってください。

▶ **Please stop there.**
   Soko-de tomete kudasai. そこで　とめてください。
   (Soe-koe day toe-may-tay kuu-dah-sie)

▶ **Please stop at the next intersection.**
   Tsugi-no kōsaten-de tomete kudasai.
   (T'sue-ghee no koe-sah-ten day toe-may-teh kuu-dah-sie)
   つぎの　こうさてんで　とめてください。

▶ **Please wait.**
   Matte-ite kudasai. まっていて　ください。
   (Mot-tay ee-tay kuu-dah-sie)

When asking a taxi driver to wait, Japanese say "please be waiting."

▶ **I'll be back in two or three minutes.**
   Ni-san-pun-de modotte kimasu.
   (Nee-sahn poon day moe-doe-tay kee-mahss)
   にさんぷんで　もどって　きます。

AT A HOTEL

hotel	*hoteru (hoe-tay-rue)* ホテル
reservations	*yoyaku (yoe-yah-kuu)* よやく
front desk	*furonto (who-rohn-toe)* フロント
bell desk	*beru-desuku* ベルデスク
	(bay-rue dess-kuu)
cashier	*kaikei (kie-kay)* かいけい
room rate	*shukuhaku-ryō* しゅくはくりょう
	(shuu-kuu-hah-kuu re-yoe)

service charge	*sābisu-ryō* サービスりょう *(sah-bee-suu re-yoe)*
business	*bijinesu (bee-jee-nay-suu)* ビジネス or *shigoto (she-go-toe)* しごと
holiday	*kyūka (queue-kah)* きゅうか
single	*shinguru (sheen-guu-rue)* シングル
double	*daburu (dah-buu-rue)* ダブル
twin	*tsuin (t'sue-ween)* ツイン
bed	*beddo (bed-doe)* ベッド
room	*rūmu (ruu-muu)* ルーム or *heya (hay-yah)* へや
large	*ōkii (oh-key)* おおきい
small	*chiisai (cheee-sie)* ちいさい
clean	*kirei-na (kee-ray na)* きれいな
room number	*rūmu-nanbā* ルームナンバー *(ruu-muu nahm-bah)* or *heya-bangō* へやばんごう *(hay-yah bahn-go)*
key	*kī (kee)* キー or *kagi (kah-ghee)* かぎ
air conditioning	*eakon (ay-ah-koen)* エアコン or *reibō (ray-boe)* れいぼう
blanket	*mōfu (moe-who)* もうふ
laundry	*sentaku-mono* せんたくもの *(sen-tah-kuu-moe-no)*
English newspaper	*eiji-shinbun* えいじしんぶん *(aa-jee sheem-boon)*
message	*messēji (mays-say-jee)* メッセージ or *kotozuke* ことづけ *(koe-toe-zuu-kay)*
check-in	*chekku-in* チェックイン *(check-kuu-een)*

checkout	*chekku-auto* チェックアウト (check-kuu-ow-toe)
luggage	*nimotsu* (nee-moe-t'sue) にもつ
porter	*bōi* (boe-ee) ボーイ or *pōtā* (poe-tah) ポーター
tip	*chippu* (chip-puu) チップ
elevator	*erebētā* (eh-ray-bay-tah) エレベーター
staircase	*kaidan* (kie-dahn) かいだん
emergency exit	*hijō-guchi* ひじょうぐち (he-joe guu-chee)
coffee shop	*kōhī-shoppu* コーヒーショップ (koe-hee shope-puu) or *kissa-ten* (kees-sah-ten) きっさてん
beauty parlor	*biyōin* (bee-yoe een) びよういん
restaurant	*resutoran* (ray-sue-toe-run) レストラン
Chinese restaurant	*chūka-ryōri-ten* ちゅうかりょうりてん (chuu-kah rio-ree ten)
drugstore	*yakkyoku* (yahk-k'yoe-kuu) やっきょく
shopping arcade	*ākēdo* (ah-kay-e-doe) アーケード or *shōten-gai* (show-ten-guy) しょうてんがい

▶ **My name is Jones. I have a reservation.**
   Jōnzu-desu. Yoyaku-shite arimasu.
   (Joan-zuu dess. Yoe-yah-kuu sshtay ah-ree-mahss)
   ジョーンズです。 よやくして　あります。

▶ **What is my room number?**
   Watashi-no heya-wa nan-gō-shitsu-desu-ka.
   (Wah-tah-she no hay-yah wah nahn go-she-t'sue dess kah)
   わたしの　へやは　なんごうしつですか。

▶ **Do you have a single?**
  Shinguru-ga arimasu-ka. シングルが　ありますか。
  (Sheen-guu-ruu gah ah-ree-mahss kah)

▶ **How about a double?**
  Daburu-wa dō-desu-ka. ダブルは　どうですか。
  (Dah-buu-ruu wah doe dess kah)

▶ **How much is the room rate?**
  Ryōkin-wa ikura-desu-ka. りょうきんは　いくらですか。
  (Re-yoe-keen wah ee-kuu-rah dess kah)

▶ **What time is checkout?**
  Chekku-auto-wa nan-ji-desu-ka.
  (Check-kuu ow-toe wah nahn jee dess kah)
  チェックアウトは　なんじですか。

▶ **This room is too small.**
  Kono heya-wa chiisa-sugimasu.
  (Koe-no hay-yah wah cheee-sah suu-ghee-mahss)
  このへやは　ちいさすぎます。

▶ **Do you have a larger one?**
  Motto ōkii-no-wa arimasen-ka.
  (Moat-toe oh-key no wah ah-ree-mah-sen kah)
  もっと　おおきいのは　ありませんか。

Note that a negative question is often used when asking if the listener has something.

▶ **What time does the coffee shop open?**
Kōhī-shoppu-wa nan-ji-ni akimasu-ka.
(Koe-hee shope-puu wah nahn-jee nee ah-kee-mahss kah)
コーヒーショップは　なんじに　あきますか。

▶ **Where is the coffee shop?**
Kōhī-shoppu-wa doko-desu-ka.
(Koe-hee shope-puu wah doe-koe dess kah)
コーヒーショップは　どこですか。

▶ **Please clean up my room.**
Heya-o sōji-shite kudasai.
(Hay-yah oh soh-jee ssh-tay kuu-dah-sie)
へやを　そうじして　ください。

▶ **I would like another blanket, please.**
Mōfu-o mō-ichi-mai onegai-shimasu.
(Moe-who oh moe ee-chee-my oh-nay-guy-she-mahss)
もうふを　もういちまい　おねがいします。

▶ **Please give me a wake-up call at 6 o'clock.**
Roku-ji-ni mōningu-kōru-o onegai-shimasu.
(Roe-kuu jee nee moe-neengu-koe-rue oh oh-nay-guy-she-mahss)
ろくじに　モーニングコールを　おねがいします。

▶ **Are there any messages for me?**
Nanika kotozuke-ga arimasen-ka.
(Nah-nee kah koe-toe-zuu-kay gah ah-ree-mah-sen kah)
なにか　ことづけが　ありませんか。

▶ **I have some laundry** (for pick up).
Sentaku-mono-o onegai-shimasu.
(Sen-tah-kuu-moe-no oh oh-nay-guy-she-mahss)
せんたくものを　おねがいします。

▶ **When will it be ready?**
Itsu-goro dekimasu-ka. いつごろ　できますか。
(Eet-sue go-roe day-kee-mahss kah)

▶ **Can you extend my reservations?**
Yoyaku-o nobasu-koto-wa dekimasen-ka.
(Yoe-yah-kuu oh no-bah-suu koe-toe wah day-kee-mah-sen kah)
よやくを　のばすことは　できませんか。

Note that a negative question is also used when asking for a favor.

▶ **I would like to stay for three more days.**
Ato mikka tomaritai-n-desu-kedo.
(Ah-toe meek-kah toe-mah-ree-tien dess kay-doe)
あと　みっか　とまりたいんですけど。

▶ **Please call me a taxi.**
Takushī-o yonde kudasai. タクシーを　よんで　ください。
(Tock-she oh yoan-day kuu-dah-sie)

▶ **Can you recommend a Chinese restaurant?**
O-susume-no chūka-ryōri-ten-wa arimasen-ka.
(Oh-sue-sue-may no chuu-kah rio-ree-ten wah ah-ree-mah-sen kah)
おすすめの　ちゅうかりょうりてんは　ありませんか。

▶ **How far is it from the hotel?**
   Hoteru-kara dono-kurai-desu-ka.
   (Hoe-tay-rue kah-rah doe-no kuu-rye dess kah)
   ホテルから　どのくらいですか。

▶ **Is there a pharmacy near the hotel?**
   Hoteru-no-chikaku-ni yakkyoku-wa arimasen-ka.
   (Hoe-tay-rue no chee-kah-kuu nee yack-k'yoe-kuu wah ah-ree-mah-sen kah)
   ホテルの　ちかくに　やっきょくは　ありませんか。

▶ **Can I walk there from the hotel?**
   Hoteru-kara soko-made aruite ikemasu-ka.
   (Hoe-tay-rue kah-rah so-koe mah-day ah-rue-ee-tay ee-kay-mahss kah)
   ホテルから　そこまで　あるいて　いけますか。

▶ **Where is your business service center?**
   Bijinesu-sābisu-sentā-wa doko-desu-ka.
   (Beejee-nay-suu sah-bee-suu sen-tah wah doe-koe dess kah)
   ビジネス・サービス・センターは　どこですか。

▶ **Do you have secretarial service?**
   Hisho-no sābisu-wa arimasen-ka.
   (He-show no sah-bee-suu wah ah-ree-mah-sen kah)
   ひしょの　サービスは　ありませんか。

ASKING QUESTIONS

country	*kuni (kuu-nee)* くに
Australia	*Ōsutoraria* オーストラリア *(oh-sue-toe-rah-ree-ah)*
Canada	*Kanada (kah-nah-dah)* カナダ
China	*Chūgoku (chuu-go-kuu)* ちゅうごく
England	*Ingurando (een-goo-run-doe)* イングランド
France	*Furansu (who-run-suu)* フランス
Germany	*Doitsu (doe-e-t'suu)* ドイツ
Ireland	*Airurando* アイルランド *(ah-ee-rue-run-doe)*
Italy	*Itaria (ee-tah-ree-ah)* イタリア
Japan	*Nihon (nee-hoan)* にほん
Korea	*Kankoku (Kahn-koe-kuu)* かんこく
New Zealand	*Nyūjīrando* ニュージーランド *(ne-yuu-jee-run-doe)*
Scotland	*Sukottorando* スコットランド *(sue-koet-toe-run-doe)*
Singapore	*Singapōru* シンガポール *(sheen-gah-poe-rue)*
Spain	*Supein (sue-pain)* スペイン
U.S.A.	*Amerika (ah-may-ree-kah)* アメリカ
U.K.	*Igirisu (ee-ghee-ree-sue)* イギリス
Wales	*Uēruzu (u-eh-rue-zoo)* ウエールズ
nationality	*kokuseki (koe-kuu-say-kee)* こくせき

When referring to one's own nationality, add *-jin (jean)* じ
ん after a country name (e.g. *Amerika-jin* American). When
referring to someone else's nationality, add *-no-kata (-no
kah-tah)* のかた after a country name (e.g. *Amerika-no-kata*
American).

language	*kotoba* (koe-toe-bah) ことば
Chinese	*Chūgoku-go* (chuu-go-kuu-go) ちゅうごくご
English	*Eigo* (aa-go) えいご
French	*Furansu-go* (who-run-suu-go) フランスご
German	*Doitsu-go* (doe-e-t'suu-go) ドイツご
Italian	*Itaria-go* (ee-tah-ree-ah-go) イタリアご
Japanese	*Nihon-go* (nee-hoan-go) にほんご
Korean	*Kankoku-go* (kahn-koe-kuu-go) かんこくご
Spanish	*Supein-go* (sue-pain-go) スペインご
food/dish	*ryōri* (rio-ree) りょうり

Add *-ryōri* (rio-ree) りょうり after a country name to refer to the food of a certain country (e.g. *Itaria-ryōri* Italian food). The following terms are also used:

Chinese food	*chūka-ryōri* ちゅうかりょうり (chuu-kah rio-ree)
Japanese food	*washoku* (wah-show-koo) わしょく
Western food	*yōshoku* (yoe-show-koo) ようしょく
last name	*myōji* (m'yoh-jee) みょうじ
rank/title	*katagaki* (kah-tah-gah-kee) かたがき
section chief	*kachō* (kah-choe) かちょう
department head	*buchō* (boo-choe) ぶちょう
president	*shachō* (shah-choe) しゃちょう
meeting	*kaigi* (kie-ghee) かいぎ
leave	*demasu* (day-mahss) でます
start	*hajimemasu* はじめます (hah-jee-may mahss)

▶ **Who is it?**
Donata-desu-ka. どなたですか。
(Doe-nah-tah dess kah)

▶ **What is your last name?**
Myōji-wa nan-desu-ka. みょうじは　なんですか。
(M'yoh-jee wah nahn dess kah)

▶ **It's White.**
Howaito-desu. *(Hoe-wa-ee-toe dess)* ホワイトです。

▶ **What is your nationality?**
Kokuseki-wa dochira-desu-ka.
(Koe-kuu-say-kee wah doe-chee-rah dess kah)
こくせきは　どちらですか。

▶ **Are you English?**
Igirisu-no kata-desu-ka. イギリスの　かたですか。
(Ee-ghee-ree-sue-no kah-tah dess kah)

▶ **Yes, I am.**
Ee, sō-desu. *(Eh-eh, soh-dess)* ええ、そうです。

▶ **No, I'm American.**
Ie, Amerika-jin-desu. いえ、アメリカじんです。
(Ee-eh, Ah-may-ree-kah-jeen dess)

▶ **What is his/her rank/title?**
Ano kata-no katagaki-wa nan-desu-ka.
(Ah-no-kah-tah no kah-tah-gah-kee wah nahn dess kah)
あのかたの　かたがきは　なんですか。

▶ **It's section chief.**
  Kachō-desu. (Kah-choe dess) かちょうです。

▶ **What is buchō called in English?**
  Buchō-wa Eigo-de nan-to iimasu-ka.
  (Boo-choe wah aa-go day nahn-toe ee-mahss kah)
  ぶちょうは　えいごで　なんと　いいますか。

▶ **When are we/you/they leaving?**
  Itsu demasu-ka. いつ　でますか。
  (Eet-sue day-mahss kah)

Note that the "we/you/they" is understood from the context.

▶ **When shall we start?**
  Itsu hajimemashō-ka. いつ　はじめましょうか。
  (Eet-sue hah-jee-may mah-show kah)

▶ **How shall we do it?**
  Dono yō-ni shimashō-ka.
  (Doh-noh yoe-nee she-mah-show kah)
  どのように　しましょうか。

▶ **Will you/they come soon?**
  Sugu kimasu-ka. すぐ　きますか。
  (Sue-guu kee-mahss kah)

▶ **Will you/they return soon?**
  Sugu modotte kimasu-ka. すぐ　もどって　きますか。
  (Sue-guu moe-doet-tay kee-mahss kah)

▶ **Is Mr. Tachibana coming to the meeting?**
Tachibana-san-wa kaigi-ni kimasu-ka.
(Tah-chee-bah-nah-sahn wah kie-ghee nee kee-mahss kah)
たちばなさんは　かいぎに　きますか。

▶ **Do I/we/you/they have to go now?**
Ima sugu ikanakute-wa ikemasen-ka.
(Ee-mah suu-guu ee-kah-nah-koo-tay wah ee-kay-mah-sen kah)
いますぐ　いかなくては　いけませんか。

▶ **What would you like to eat?**
Nani-o tabemasu-ka. (lit. What will you eat?)
(Nah-nee oh tah-bay-mahss kah)
なにを　たべますか。
Nani-o tabemashō-ka. (lit. What shall we eat?)
(Nah-nee oh tah-bay-mah-show kah)
なにを　たべましょうか。

Note that when asking the listener what he/she would like to do, Japanese do not use the desiderative form in business or in formal situations. Instead, they say "what will you ...?" or "what shall we ...?" in a question with an interrogative word and "won't you ...?" in a question with no interrogative word.

▶ **Would you like to eat Japanese food?**
Washoku-o tabemasen-ka. わしょくを　たべませんか。
(Wah-show-koo oh tah-bay-mah-sen kah)

▶ **How about Western food?**
Yōshoku-wa dō-desu-ka. ようしょくは　どうですか。
(Yoe-show-kuu wah doe-dess kah)

GOING SOMEWHERE

bar	*bā (bah)* バー
cabaret	*kyabarē* キャバレー *(kʹyah-bah-ray)*
pub	*pabu (pah-boo)* パブ
movie	*eiga (a-eegah)* えいが
taxi	*takushī (tock-she)* タクシー
subway	*chikatetsu* ちかてつ *(chee-kah-tet-sue)*
bus	*basu (bah-sue)* バス
sushi restaurant	*sushi-ya (suu-shee yah)* すしや
stroll / walk	*sanpo (sahm-poe)* さんぽ
sightseeing	*kankō (kahn-koe)* かんこう
appointment	*yakusoku (yahk-soe-kuu)* やくそく
far (distant)	*tōi (toh-ee)* とおい
close (nearby)	*chikai (chee-kie)* ちかい

▶ **I want to go somewhere this evening.**
Konban doko-ka-ni ikitai-desu.
(Kome-bahn doe-koe kah nee ee-kee-tie dess)
こんばん　どこかに　いきたいです。

▶ **Would you like to go with me?**
Issho-ni ikimasen-ka. いっしょに　いきませんか。
(Ees-show nee ee-kee-mah-sen kah)

▶ **Oh, that's a good idea.**
A, ii-desu-ne. あ、いいですね。
(Ah, ee-dess nay)

▶ **I'm afraid not this evening.**
Sumimasen, konban-wa chotto.
(Sue-me-mah-sen kome-bahm wah choat-toe)
すみません、こんばんは ちょっと。

▶ **I am sorry, I have an appointment.**
Sumimasen, yakusoku-ga aru-n-desu.
(Sue-me-mah-sen yahk-soe-kuu gah ah-ruen-dess)
すみません、やくそくが あるんです。

▶ **Where would you like to go?**
Doko-ni ikimashō-ka. どこに いきましょうか。
(Doe-koe nee ee-kee-mah-show kah)

▶ **Let's go to a cabaret.**
Kyabarē-ni ikimashō. キャバレーに いきましょう。
(K'yah-bah-ray nee ee-kee-mah-show)

▶ **Let's take a walk.**
Sanpo-shimashō. さんぽしましょう。
(Sahm-poe she-mah-show)

▶ **I'd like to go to a sushi restaurant.**
Sushi-ya-ni ikitai-desu. すしやに いきたいです。
(Sue-she yah nee ee-kee-tie dess)

▶ **I'd like to do a little sightseeing.**
Sukoshi kanko-ga shitai-desu.
(Sue-koe-she kahn-koe-ga she-tie dess)
すこし かんこうが したいです。

► **Is it far from here?**
 Koko-kara tōi-desu-ka. ここから　とおいですか。
 (Koe-koe kah-rah toh-ee dess kah)

► **Is it near here?**
 Koko-kara chikai-desu-ka. ここから　ちかいですか。
 (Koe-koe kah-rah chee-kai dess kah)

► **Is it near a subway station?**
 Chikatetsu-no eki-kara chikai-desu-ka.
 (Chee-kah-tet-sue no a-kee kah-rah chee-kie dess kah)
 ちかてつの　えきから　ちかいですか。

► **Shall we go by subway?**
 Chikatetsu-de ikimashō-ka.
 (Chee-kah-tet-sue day ee-kie-mah-show kah)
 ちかてつで　いきましょうか。

► **Let's go by taxi.**
 Takushī-de ikimashō. タクシーで　いきましょう。
 (Tock-she day ee-kie-mah-show)

► **Let's walk there.**
 Aruite ikimashō. あるいて　いきましょう。
 (Ah-rue-ee-tay ee-kie-mah-show)

THE CARDINAL NUMBERS

Numbers are vital to communication even on the most basic
level. In Japanese there are two sets of cardinal numbers from
1 through 10, making it a bit more complicated than usual.

One set was borrowed from China and the other set is native Japanese. From 11 on, the imported Chinese numbering system is used.

Japanese

1   *hitotsu* (he-toe-t'sue) ひとつ
2   *futatsu* (who-tah-t'sue) ふたつ
3   *mittsu* (meet-sue) みっつ
4   *yottsu* (yoat-sue) よっつ
5   *itsutsu* (ee-t'sue-t'sue) いつつ
6   *muttsu* (moot-sue) むっつ
7   *nanatsu* (nah-naht-sue) ななつ
8   *yattsu* (yaht-sue) やっつ
9   *kokonotsu* (koe-ko-no-t'sue) ここのつ
10   *tō* (toe) とお

Chinese

1   *ichi* (ee-chee) いち
2   *ni* (nee) に
3   *san* (sahn) さん
4   *shi* (she) し or *yon* (yoan) よん
5   *go* (go) ご
6   *roku* (roe-kuu) ろく
7   *shichi* (she-chee) しち or *nana* (nah-nah) なな
8   *hachi* (hah-chee) はち
9   *ku* (kuu) く or *kyū* (queue) きゅう
10   *jū* (juu) じゅう

The criterion for using these two sets of numbers is fairly clear-cut. The Japanese set is generally used when referring to units of 9 or under. For example, if you want two orders of French fries, you would not use *ni* (nee) に, but *futatsu (who-*

tah-t̄sue) ふたつ ***Furaido- poteto-o futatsu kudasai*** *(who-rie-doh- poe-tey-toh oh who-tah-t̄sue kuu-dah-sie)* フライドポテト を　ふたつください。 "I'll have two French fries, please."

There are occasions when numbers from 1-9 use the Chinese numerals. These will be explained shortly in "Counting Things."

From 11 on, all numbers are combinations of the Chinese set: 11 is 10 + 1, 22 is 2 x 10 + 2, 356 is 3 x 100 + 5 x 10 + 6, and so on:

11 ***jū-ichi*** *(juu-ee-chee)* じゅういち
12 ***jū-ni*** *(juu-nee)* じゅうに
13 ***jū-san*** *(juu-sahn)* じゅうさん
14 ***jū-shi*** *(juu-she)* じゅうし or
   jū-yon *(juu-yoan)* じゅうよん
15 ***jū-go*** *(juu-go)* じゅうご
16 ***jū-roku*** *(juu-roe-kuu)* じゅうろく
17 ***jū-shichi*** *(juu-she-chee)* じゅうしち or
   jū-nana *(juu-nah-nah)* じゅうなな*
18 ***jū-hachi*** *(juu-hah-chee)* じゅうはち
19 ***jū-ku*** *(juu-kuu)* じゅうく or
   jū-kyū *(juu-queue)* じゅうきゅう
20 ***ni-jū*** *(nee-juu)* にじゅう
21 ***ni-jū-ichi*** *(nee-juu-ee-chee)* にじゅういち
22 ***ni-jū-ni*** *(nee-juu-nee)* にじゅうに
23 ***ni-jū-san*** *(nee-juu-sahn)* にじゅうさん
24 ***ni-jū-shi*** *(nee-juu-she)* にじゅうし or
   ni-jū-yon *(nee-juu-yoan)* にじゅうよん
25 ***ni-jū-go*** *(nee-juu-go)* にじゅうご
26 ***ni-jū-roku*** *(nee-juu-roe-kuu)* にじゅうろく
27 ***ni-jū-shichi*** *(nee-juu-she-chee)* にじゅうしち or
   ni-jū-nana *(nee-juu-nah-nah)* にじゅうなな*

28	***ni-jū-hachi*** *(nee-juu-hah-chee)* にじゅうはち
29	***ni-jū-ku*** *(nee-juu-kuu)* にじゅうく or
	ni-jū-kyū *(nee-juu-queue)* にじゅうきゅう
30	***san-jū*** *(sahn-juu)* さんじゅう
40	***yon-jū*** *(yoan-juu)* よんじゅう
50	***go-jū*** *(go-juu)* ごじゅう
60	***roku-jū*** *(roe-kuu-juu)* ろくじゅう
70	***nana-jū*** *(nah-nah-juu)* ななじゅう* or
	shichi-jū *(she-chee-juu)* しちじゅう
80	***hachi-jū*** *(hah-chee-juu)* はちじゅう
90	***kyū-jū*** *(queue-juu)* きゅうじゅう

*Note that **nanatsu** *(nah-naht-sue)* ななつ is frequently abbreviated to **nana** *(nah-nah)* なな and used with the Chinese set.

100	***hyaku*** *(h'yah-kuu)* ひゃく
101	***hyaku-ichi*** *(h'yah-kuu-ee-chee)* ひゃくいち
102	***hyaku-ni*** *(h'yah-kuu-nee)* ひゃくに
103	***hyaku-san*** *(h'yah-kuu-sahn)* ひゃくさん
110	***hyaku-jū*** *(h'yah-kuu-juu)* ひゃくじゅう
111	***hyaku-jū-ichi*** ひゃくじゅういち
	(h'yah-kuu-juu-ee-chee)
112	***hyaku-jū-ni*** ひゃくじゅうに
	(h'yah-kuu-juu-nee)
120	***hyaku-ni-jū*** ひゃくにじゅう
	(h'yah-kuu-nee-juu)
121	***hyaku-ni-jū-ichi*** ひゃくにじゅういち
	(h'yah-kuu-nee-juu-ee-chee)
130	***hyaku-san-jū*** ひゃくさんじゅう
	(h'yah-kuu-sahn-juu)
200	***ni-hyaku*** *(nee-h'yah)* にひゃく

300	*san-byaku* (sahm-b'yah-ku) さんびゃく*
400	*yon-hyaku* (yoan-h'yah-kuu) よんひゃく
500	*go-hyaku* (go-h'yah-kuu) ごひゃく
600	*rop-pyaku* (rope-p'yah-kuu) ろっぴゃく*
700	*nana-hyaku* (nah-nah-h'yah-kuu) ななひゃく
800	*hap-pyaku* (hop-p'yah-kuu) はっぴゃく*
900	*kyū-hyaku* (queue-h'yah-kuu) きゅうひゃく
1,000	*sen* (sen) せん
1,001	*sen-ichi* (sen-ee-chee) せんいち
1,010	*sen-jū* (sen-juu) せんじゅう
1,100	*sen-hyaku* (sen-h'yah-kuu) せんひゃく
2,000	*ni-sen* (nee-sen) にせん
3,000	*san-zen* (sahn zen) さんぜん*
4,000	*yon-sen* (yoan sen) よんせん
5,000	*go-sen* (go-sen) ごせん
6,000	*roku-sen* (roe-kuu-sen) ろくせん
7,000	*nana-sen* (nah-nah-sen) ななせん
8,000	*has-sen* (hos-sen) はっせん*
9,000	*kyū-sen* (queue-sen) きゅうせん

*Note occasional euphonic changes to make pronunciation easier.

10,000	*ichi-man* (ee-chee-mahn) いちまん
11,000	*ichi-man-is-sen* いちまんいっせん (ee-chee-mahn-ees-sen)*
12,000	*ichi-man-ni-sen* いちまんにせん (ee-chee-mahn-nee-sen)
20,000	*ni-man* (nee-mahn) にまん
21,000	*ni-man-is-sen* にまんいっせん (nee-mahn-ees-sen)*
30,000	*san-man* (sahn-mahn) さんまん

40,000	***yon-man*** *(yoan-mahn)*	よんまん
50,000	***go-man*** *(go-mahn)*	ごまん
60,000	***roku-man*** *(roe-kuu-mahn)*	ろくまん
70,000	***nana-man*** *(nah-nah-mahn)*	ななまん
80,000	***hachi-man*** *(hah-chee-mahn)*	はちまん
90,000	***kyū-man*** *(queue-mahn)*	きゅうまん
100,000	***jū-man*** *(juu-mahn)*	じゅうまん
150,000	***jū-go-man*** *(juu-go-mahn)*	じゅうごまん
200,000	***ni-jū-man*** *(nee-juu-mahn)*	にじゅうまん
300,000	***san-jū-man*** *(sahn-juu-mahn)*	さんじゅうまん
400,000	***yon-jū-man*** *(yoan-juu-mahn)*	よんじゅうまん
500,000	***go-jū-man*** *(go-juu-mahn)*	ごじゅうまん
600,000	***roku-jū-man*** *(roe-kuu-juu-mahn)*	ろくじゅうまん
700,000	***nana-jū-man*** *(nah-nah-juu-mahn)*	ななじゅうまん
800,000	***hachi-jū-man*** *(hah-chee-juu-mahn)*	はちじゅうまん
900,000	***kyū-jū-man*** *(queue-juu-mahn)*	きゅうじゅうまん
1,000,000	***hyaku-man*** *(h'yah-kuu-mahn)*	ひゃくまん
2,000,000	***ni-hyaku-man*** *(nee-h'yah-kuu-mahn)*	にひゃくまん
3,000,000	***san-byaku-man*** *(sahn-b'yah-kuu-mahn)*	さんびゃくまん
4,000,000	***yon-hyaku-man*** *(yoan-h'ya-kuu-mahn)*	よんひゃくまん
5,000,000	***go-hyaku-man*** *(go-h'ya-kuu-mahn)*	ごひゃくまん

6,000,000	*rop-pyaku-man* ろっぴゃくまん
	(rope-p'ya-kuu-mahn)
7,000,000	*nana-hyaku-man* ななひゃくまん
	(nah-nah-h'yah-kuu-mahn)
8,000,000	*hap-pyaku-man* はっぴゃくまん
	(hop-p'ya-kuu-mahn)
9,000,000	*kyū-hyaku-man* きゅうひゃくまん
	(queue-h'yah-kuu-mahn)
10,000,000	*is-sen-man (ees-sen-mahn)* いっせんまん*
15,000,000	*is-sen-go-hyaku-man*
	(ees-sen go-h'ya-kuu-mahn)
	いっせんごひゃくまん*

*Note that *is-* *(ees)* いっ is added to *sen (sen)* せん when *sen (sen)* せん is preceded by other digits and/or followed by *man (mahn)* まん .

THE ORDINAL NUMBERS

Converting cardinal numbers to ordinal numbers is simple. All you do is add *ban-me (bahm-may)* ばんめ to the cardinal numbers. In usage, *ban-me (bahm-may)* ばんめ is often shortened to *ban (bahn)* ばん. For example:

▶ **What number are you?**
Anata-wa nan-ban-desu-ka. あなたは　なんばんですか。
(Ah-nah-tah wah nahm bahn dess kah)

▶ **I'm number five.**
Go-ban-desu. (Go-bahn dess) ごばんです。

1st	*ichi-ban-me (ee-chee-bahm-may)* いちばんめ or
	ichi-ban (ee-chee-bahn) いちばん
2nd	*ni-ban-me (nee-bahm-may)* にばんめ or
	ni-ban (nee-bahn) にばん
3rd	*san-ban-me (sahm-bahm-may)* さんばんめ or
	san-ban (sahm-bahn) さんばん
4th	*yon-ban-me (yoam-bahm-may)* よんばんめ or
	yon-ban (yoam-bahn) よんばん
5th	*go-ban-me (go-bahm-may)* ごばんめ or
	go-ban (go-bahn) ごばん
6th	*roku-ban-me* ろくばんめ
	(roe-kuu-bahm-may) or
	roku-ban (roe-kuu-bahn) ろくばん
7th	*nana-ban-me (nah-nah-bahm-may)* ななばんめ or
	nana-ban (nah-nah-bahn) ななばん
8th	*hachi-ban-me* はちばんめ
	(hah-chee-bahm-may) or
	hachi-ban (hah-chee-bahn) はちばん
9th	*kyū-ban-me (queue-bahm-may)* きゅうばんめ or
	kyū-ban (queue-bahn) きゅうばん
10th	*jū-ban-me (juu-bahm-may)* じゅうばんめ or
	jū-ban (juu-bahn) じゅうばん
11th	*jū-ichi-ban-me* じゅういちばんめ
	(juu-ee-chee-bahm-may) or
	jū-ichi-ban (juu-ee-chee-bahn) じゅういちばん
20th	*ni-jū-ban-me* にじゅうばんめ
	(nee-juu-bahm-may) or
	ni-jū-ban (nee-juu-bahn) にじゅうばん
50th	*go-jū-ban-me* ごじゅうばんめ
	(go-juu-bahm-may) or
	go-jū-ban (go-juu-bahn) ごじゅうばん

The prefix *dai (die)* だい may be put in front of ordinal numbers to emphasize the order of things. For example: "the first one" could be *ichi-ban-me (ee-chee-bahm-may)* いちばんめ or *dai-ichi-ban-me (dai-ee-chee-bahm-may)* だいいちばんめ. When the ordinal number qualifies a noun, the particle *no (no)* の is used to connect them. "The second person" is *ni-ban-me-no hito (nee-bahm-may no he-toe)* にばんめの ひと.

COUNTING THINGS

A special set of numeratives is used when counting things and people in Japanese. Altogether there are over 25 such numeratives. Some of the commonly used ones are:

- *hai (hie)* はい used to designate cups or glassfuls of water or other liquids, spoonfuls of sugar, salt, etc., bowlfuls of rice, and so on.
- *hiki (hee-kee)* ひき used when counting animals, fish and insects;
- *hon (hoan)* ほん used when counting long, slender objects, such as pencils, trees, chopsticks, poles, legs, fingers, and so on;
- *ko (koe)* こ used when counting relatively small, roundish objects, such as apples, balls, erasers, and so on;
- *mai (my)* まい used when counting flat, thin objects, such as paper, sheets, dishes, boards, trays, and so on;
- *satsu (sot-sue)* さつ used when counting books and other bound objects.

A numerative is put immediately after the word and the particle that follows, when it modifies the subject or the direct object. Otherwise, *no (no)* の is added after the numerative and it is put in front of the modified noun.

	Hai (はい)	Hiki (ひき)	Hon (ほん)	Ko (こ)	Mai (まい)	Satsu (さつ)
1	Ip-pai* いっぱい	Ip-piki* いっぴき	Ip-pon* いっぽん	Ik-ko* いっこ	Ichi-mai いちまい	Is-satsu* いっさつ
2	Ni-hai にはい	Ni-hiki にひき	Ni-hon にほん	Ni-ko にこ	Ni-mai にまい	Ni-satsu にさつ
3	San-bai* さんばい	San-biki* さんびき	San-bon* さんぼん	San-ko さんこ	San-mai さんまい	San-satsu さんさつ
4	Yon-hai よんはい	Yon-hiki よんひき	Yon-hon よんほん	Yon-ko よんこ	Yon-mai よんまい	Yon-satsu よんさつ
5	Go-hai ごはい	Go-hiki ごひき	Go-hon ごほん	Go-ko ごこ	Go-mai ごまい	Go-satsu ごさつ
6	Rop-pai* ろっぱい	Rop-piki* ろっぴき	Rop-pon* ろっぽん	Rok-ko* ろっこ	Roku-mai ろくまい	Roku-satsu ろくさつ
7	Nana-hai ななはい	Nana-hiki ななひき	Nana-hon ななほん	Nana-ko ななこ	Nana-mai ななまい	Nana-satsu ななさつ
8	Hap-pai* はっぱい	Hap-piki* はっぴき	Hap-pon* はっぽん	Hak-ko* はっこ	Hachi-mai はちまい	Has-satsu* はっさつ
9	Kyū-hai きゅうはい	Kyū-hiki きゅうひき	Kyū-hon きゅうほん	Kyū-ho きゅうこ	Kyū-mai きゅうまい	Kyū-satsu きゅうさつ
10	Jup-pai* じゅっぱい	Jup-piki* じゅっぴき	Jup-pon* じゅっぽん	Juk-ko* じゅっこ	Juu-mai じゅうまい	Jus-satsu* じゅっさつ
How many	Nan-bai* なんばい	Nan-biki* なんびき	Nan-bon* なんぼん	Nan-ko なんこ	Nan-mai なんまい	Nan-satsu なんさつ

*Note occasional euphonic changes to make pronunciation easier.

► **We have two dogs in our house.**
  Uchi-ni-wa inu-ga ni-hiki imasu.
  *(*lit. Two dogs are in our house.*)*
  (Uu-chee nee wah ee-nuu gah nee-hee-kee ee-mahss)
  うちには　いぬが　にひき　います。

► **Could we have three bottles of beer, please?**
  Bīru-o san-bon onegai-shimasu.
  (Bee-rue oh sham-boan oh-nay-guy-she-mahss)
  ビールを　さんぼん　おねがいします。

► **I bought four magazines at a kiosk.**
  Kiosuku-de zasshi-o yon-satsu kaimashita.
  (Key-oh-sue-koo day zahs-she oh yoan-sot-sue kei-mah-sshtah)
  キオスクで　ざっしを　よんさつ　かいました。

When counting or ordering something like hamburgers, which have a more or less indefinite shape, it is common to use the Japanese set of numerals (i.e. *hitotsu*, *futatsu*, *mittsu*, and so on). For example,

► **Two hamburgers, please.**
  Hanbāgā-o futatsu kudasai.
  (Hahm-bah-gah oh who-tah-t́sue kuu-dah-sie)
  ハンバーガーを　ふたつ　ください。

If you don't know the correct numerative for whatever is concerned, just use numbers from the Japanese set for **1-10** and from the Chinese set for **11** onwards. It may sound odd but you will be understood.

COUNTING PEOPLE

There are two numeratives, *nin (neen)* にん and *mei (may)* めい, for counting people, and special words for counting one person and two people. Taking these two special words first, they are *hitori (he-toe-ree)* ひとり, meaning one person, and *futari (who-tah-ree)* ふたり, meaning two people. These special words are almost always used instead of *nin (neen)* にん when referring to one person or two people. *Ichi-mei (ee-chee-may)* いちめい and *ni-mei (nee-may)* にめい may be used in formal situations.)

The *mei (may)* めい numerative sounds more formal and more polite than the *nin (neen)* にん numerative, so is exclusively used, for example, when counting the number of people in dining groups arriving at restaurants. The host or waiter will commonly ask each new party or group that appears, *nan-mei-sama-desu-ka (nahn-may sahmah dess ka)* なんめいさまですか or "how many people?"

In responding to this question, it is common to use *hitori (he-toe-ree)* ひとり or *futari (who-tah-ree)* ふたり if there is one or two, and the numerative *nin (neen)* にん if there is more, e.g. *san-nin-desu (sahn-neen dess)* さんにんです or "three people," and *roku-nin-desu (roe-kuu-neen dess)* ろくにんです or "six people."

In all general references to three or more people the *nin (neen)* にん numerative is used, e.g. *go-nin (go-neen)* ごにん "five people," *jū-nin (juu-neen)* じゅうにん "ten people."

Note that the Chinese set of numbers must be used with *nin (neen)* にん and *mei (may)* めい, with the exception of "seven people" which can be either *shichi-nin (she-chee-neen)* しちにん and *shichi-mei (she-chee-may)* しちめい, or *nana-nin (nah-nah-neen)* ななにん and *nana-mei (nah-nah-may)* ななめい.

► **I have two daughters.**
Musume-ga futari imasu. むすめが　ふたりいます。
(Muu-sue-may gah who-tah-ree ee-mahss)

► **I/We have reservations for five people.**
Go-nin-de yoyaku shite imasu.
(Go-neen day yoe-yah-kuu ssh-tay ee-mahss)
ごにんで　よやく　しています。

TIME FRAMES

day before yesterday	*ototoi (oh-toe-toy)* おととい
yesterday	*kinō (kee-no-oh)* きのう
today	*kyō (k'yoe)* きょう
tomorrow	*ashita (ah-ssh-tah)* あした
day after tomorrow	*asatte (ah-sot-tay)* あさって
morning	*asa (ah-sah)* あさ
noon/ afternoon	*hiru (he-rue)* ひる
early evening	*yūgata (yuu-gah-tah)* ゆうがた
evening	*ban (bahn)* ばん
night	*yoru (yoe-rue)* よる
in the morning/ a.m.	*gozen (go-zen)* ごぜん
in the afternoon/ p.m.	*gogo (go-go)* ごご
yesterday morning	*kinō-no asa* きのうの　あさ *(kee-no-oh no ah-sah)*
yesterday afternoon	*kinō-no gogo* きのうの　ごご *(kee-no-oh no go-go)*

last evening/ night	*yūbe (you-bay)* ゆうべ or *kinō-no yoru* きのうの　よる *(kee-no-oh no yoe-rue)*
this morning	*kesa (kay-sah)* けさ
this afternoon	*kyō-no gogo* きょうの　ごご *(k'yoe no go-go)*
this evening	*konban (kome-bahn)* こんばん
tonight	*kon'ya (kone-yah)* こんや
tomorrow morning	*ashita-no asa* あしたの　あさ *(ah-ssh-tah no ah-sah)*
tomorrow afternoon	*ashita-no gogo* あしたの　ごご *(ah-ssh-tah no go-go)*
tomorrow evening	*ashita-no ban* あしたの　ばん *(ah-ssh-tah no bahn)*
tomorrow night	*ashita-no yoru* あしたの　よる *(ah-ssh-tah no yoe-rue)*
every day	*mainichi (my nee-chee)* まいにち
every morning	*maiasa (my ah-sah)* まいあさ
every evening/night	*maiban (my bahn)* まいばん
from today	*kyō-kara* きょうから *(k'yoe kah-rah)*
until today	*kyō-made* きょうまで *(k'yoe mah-day)*

▶ **Would you please meet me this afternoon?**
Kyō-no gogo atte moraemasen-ka.
(K'yoe no go-go aht-tay moe-rah-eh-mah-sen kah)
きょうの　ごご　あって　もらえませんか。

▶ **May I come to see you tomorrow?**
   Ashita ukagatte-mo ii-desu-ka.
   (Ah-ssh-tah uu-kah-gaht-tay moe ee-dess kah)
   あした　うかがっても　いいですか。

▶ **I really enjoyed yesterday.**
   Kinō-wa hontō-ni tanoshikatta-desu.
   (Kee-no-oh wah hoan-toe nee tah-no-she-kah-tah dess)
   きのうは　ほんとうに　たのしかったです。

▶ **Yesterday I ate sushi.**
   Kinō sushi-o tabemashita.
   (Kee-no-oh suu-she oh tah-bay-mah-sshtah)
   きのう　すしを　たべました。

▶ **Last night I went to a karaoke.**
   Yūbe karaoke-ni ikimashita.
   (Yuu-bay kah-rah-oh-kay nee ee-kee-mah-sshtah)
   ゆうべ　カラオケに　いきました。

▶ **I came to Japan the day before yesterday.**
   Ototoi Nihon-ni kimashita.
   (Oh-toe-toy nee-hoan nee kee-mah-sshtah)
   おととい　にほんに　きました。

▶ **Where are we/you going the day after tomorrow?**
   Asatte-wa doko-ni ikimasu-ka.
   (Ah-sot-tay wah doe-koe nee ee-kee-mahss kah)
   あさっては　どこに　いきますか。

▶ **I am going to Kyoto from this afternoon until tomor-row evening.**
Kyō-no gogo-kara ashita-no ban-made Kyōto-ni ikimasu.
(K'yoe no go-go kah-rah ah-ssh-tah no bahm mah-day k'yoe-toe nee ee-kee-mahss)
きょうの　ごごから　あしたの　ばんまで　きょうとに
いきます。

THE DAYS

The days of the week follow the same pattern as in English, with *yōbi (yoe-bee)* ようび meaning "day of the week."

Monday	*getsu-yōbi* げつようび	
	(get-sue-yoe-bee)	
Tuesday	*ka-yōbi (kah-yoe-bee)* かようび	
Wednesday	*sui-yōbi (suu-e-yoe-bee)* すいようび	
Thursday	*moku-yōbi* もくようび	
	(moe-kuu-yoe-bee)	
Friday	*kin-yōbi (keen-yoe-bee)* きんようび	
Saturday	*do-yōbi (doe-yoe-bee)* どようび	
Sunday	*nichi-yōbi (nee-chee-yoe-bee)* にちようび	
from	*getsu-yōbi-kara* げつようびから	
Monday	*(get-sue-yoe-bee kah-rah)*	
until	*ka-yōbi-made* かようびまで	
Tuesday	*(kah-yoe-bee mah-day)*	

▶ **What day of the week is today?**
Kyō-wa nan-yōbi-desu-ka.
(K'yoe wah nahn yoe-bee dess kah)
きょうは　なんようびですか。

▶ **It's Monday.**
Getsu-yōbi-desu. げつようびです。
(Get-sue-yoe-bee dess)

▶ **I am going to Osaka on Thursday.**
Moku-yōbi-ni Ōsaka-ni ikimasu.
(Moe-kuu-yoe-bee nee oh-sah-kah nee ee-kee-mahss)
もくようびに　おおさかに　いきます。

▶ **I will return to Tokyo on Friday afternoon.**
Kin-yōbi-no gogo Tōkyō-ni modotte kimasu.
(Keen-yoe-bee no go-go toe-k'yoe nee moe-doet-tay kee-mahss)
きんようびの　ごご　とうきょうに　もどって　きます。

▶ **On Saturday I'm going to meet a friend.**
Do-yōbi-ni tomodachi-to aimasu.
(Doe-yoe-bee nee toe-moe-dah-chee toe aye-mahss)
どようびに　ともだちと　あいます。

▶ **On Sunday evening I'm going to watch kabuki.**
Nichi-yōbi-no ban-ni kabuki-o mi-ni ikimasu.
(Nee-chee-yoe-bee no bahn nee kah-buu-kee oh me nee ee-kee-mahss)
にちようびの　ばんに　かぶきを　みに　いきます。

▶ **I have a meeting from Wednesday till Friday.**
Sui-yōbi-kara kin-yōbi-made kaigi-ga arimasu.
(Suu-e-yoe-bee kah-rah keen-yoe-bee mah-day kie-ghee gah ah-ree-mass)
すいようびから　きんようびまで　かいぎが　あります。

COUNTING DAYS

When counting days, just add *nichi (nee-chee)* にち to the appropriate number of the Chinese set, except for 2-10, 20, and any number with 4 as the last digit. The suffix *kan (kahn)* かん may be added to *nichi (nee-chee)* にち to mean "for ... days."

one day	*ichi-nichi (ee-chee nee-chee)* いちにち
two days	*futsu-ka (who-t'sue-kah)* ふつか
three days	*mik-ka (meek-kah)* みっか
four days	*yok-ka (yok-kah)* よっか
five days	*itsu-ka (ee-t'sue-kah)* いつか
six days	*mui-ka (moo-ee-kah)* むいか
seven days	*nano-ka (nah-no-kah)* なのか
eight day	*yō-ka (yoe-kah)* ようか
nine days	*kokono-ka (koe-koe-no-kah)* ここのか
ten days	*tō-ka (toe-kah)* とおか
eleven days	*jū-ichi-nichi* じゅういちにち *(juu-ee-chee nee-chee)*
fourteen days	*jū-yok-ka (juu-yok-kah)* じゅうよっか
twenty days	*hatsu-ka (hat'sue-kah)* はつか
twenty-four days	*ni-jū-yok-ka* にじゅうよっか *(nee-juu-yok-kah)*
twenty-eight days	*ni-jū-hachi-nichi* にじゅうはちにち *(nee-juu-hah-chee nee-chee)*

▶ **How many days are you going to be here?**
Koko-ni nan-nichi imasu-ka.
(Koe-koe nee nahn nee-chee ee-mahss kah)
ここに　なんにち　いますか。

▶ **I am going to be here for three days.**
Koko-ni mik-ka imasu.
(Koe-koe nee meek-kah ee-mahss)
ここに　みっかいます。

▶ **I am going to stay in Hiroshima for two days.**
Hiroshima-de futsu-ka tomarimasu.
(He-roe-she-mah day who-t'sue-kah toe-mah-ree mahss)
ひろしまで　ふつか　とまります。

▶ **How many days will it take?**
Nan-nichi-gurai kakarimasu-ka.
(Nahn nee-chee guu-rye kah-kah-ree-mahss kah)
なんにちぐらい　かかりますか。

Note that **-gurai** *(guu-rye)* ぐらい "about" is often added to an interrogative word referring duration or amount in order to avoid being too straightforward.

▶ **It will take about five days.**
Itsu-ka-gurai kakarimasu. いつかぐらい　かかります。
(Ee-t'sue-kah guu-rye kah-kah-ree-mahss)

THE WEEKS

Japanese for week is **shū** *(shoe)* しゅう. To express the concept of weeks, the suffix **kan** *(kahn)* かん is added to **shū** *(shoe)* しゅう, i.e., **shū-kan** *(shoe-kahn)* しゅうかん means "for ... week(s)."

week before last	*sensenshū* せんせんしゅう *(sen sen shuu)*
last week	*senshū (sen shuu)* せんしゅう
this week	*konshū (kone shuu)* こんしゅう
next week	*raishū (rye shuu)* らいしゅう
week after next	*saraishū* さらいしゅう *(sah rye shuu)*
weekday	*heijitsu (hay-jeet-sue)* へいじつ
weekend	*shūmatsu* しゅうまつ *(shuu-mot-sue)*
every week	*maishū (my-shuu)* まいしゅう
last Monday	*senshū-no getsu-yōbi* *(sen shuu no get-sue-yoe-bee)* せんしゅうの　げつようび
this Monday	*konshū-no getsu-yōbi* *(kone shuu no get-sue-yoe-bee)* こんしゅうの　げつようび
next Monday	*raishū-no getsu-yōbi* *(rye shuu no get-sue-yoe-bee)* らいしゅうの　げつようび
every Monday	*maishū getsu-yōbi* *(my-shuu get-sue-yoe-bee)* まいしゅう　げつようび
by next week	*raishū-made-ni* らいしゅうまでに *(rye shuu mah-day nee)*

▶ **I am going to Fukuoka this week.**
   Watashi-wa konshū fukuoka-ni ikimasu.
   (Wa-tah-she wah kone shuu who-kuu-oh-kah nee ee-kee-mahss)
   わたしは　こんしゅう　ふくおかに　いきます。

▶ **Will it be ready by next week?**
Raishū-made-ni dekimasu-ka.
(Rye shuu mah-day nee day-kee-mahss kah)
らいしゅうまでに　できますか。

▶ **Please wait until the week after next.**
Saraishū-made matte kudasai.
(Sah rye shuu mah-day mot-tay kuu-dah-sie)
さらいしゅうまで　まってください。

▶ **Please prepare the document by next Thursday.**
Raishū-no moku-yōbi-made-ni shorui-o junbi-shite kudasai.
(Rye shuu no moe-kuu yoe-bee mah-day nee show-rue-ee oh juun-bee she-tey kuu-dah-sie)
らいしゅうの　もくようびまでに　しょるいを　じゅんびしてください。

▶ **I will be in Tokyo until this Friday.**
Konshū-no kin-yōbi-made Tōkyō-ni imasu.
(Kone shuu no keen-yoe-bee mah-day toe-k'yoe nee ee-mahss)
こんしゅうの　きんようびまで　とうきょうに　います。

COUNTING WEEKS

As mentioned earlier, weeks are counted by adding a numeral prefix *shū-kan (shoe-kahn)* しゅうかん. The Chinese set of numbers is used with *shū-kan (shoe-kahn)* しゅうかん except for seven weeks.

one week	*is-shū-kan* いっしゅうかん*	(ish-shuu-kahn)
two weeks	*ni-shū-kan* にしゅうかん	(nee-shuu-kahn)
three weeks	*san-shū-kan* さんしゅうかん	(sahn-shuu-kahn)
four weeks	*yon-shū-kan* よんしゅうかん	(yoan-shuu-kahn)
five weeks	*go-shū-kan* ごしゅうかん	(go-shuu-kahn)
six weeks	*roku-shū-kan* ろくしゅうかん	(roe-kuu-shuu-kahn)
seven weeks	*nana-shū-kan* ななしゅうかん	(nah-nah-shuu-kahn)
eight weeks	*has-shū-kan* はっしゅうかん	(has-shuu-kahn)*
nine weeks	*kyū-shū-kan* きゅうしゅうかん	(queue-shuu-kahn)
ten weeks	*jus-shū-kan* じゅっしゅうかん	(juush-shuu-kahn)*
fifteen weeks	*jū-go-shū-kan* じゅうごしゅうかん	(juu-go-shuu-kahn)

*Note occasional euphonic changes to make pronunciation easier.

two weeks ago	*ni-shū-kan-mae-ni*
	(nee-shuu-kahn mah-eh nee)
	にしゅうかんまえに
two weeks later	*ni-shū-kan-go-ni*
	(nee-shuu-kahn go nee)
	にしゅうかんごに

▶ **I came to Japan one week ago.**
  Is-shū-kan-mae-ni Nihon-ni kimashita.
  (Its-shuu-kahn mah-eh nee nee-hoan nee kee-mah-sshtah)
  いっしゅうかんまえに　にほんに　きました。

▶ **I will stay here for two more weeks.**
  Ato ni-shū-kan koko-ni imasu.
  (Ah-toe nee-shuu-kahn koe-koe nee ee-mahss)
  あと　にしゅうかん　ここに　います。

▶ **I will return to my country in two weeks' time.**
  Ni-shū-kan-go-ni kikoku-shimasu.
  (Nee-shuu-kahn go nee kee-koe-kuu she-mahss)
  にしゅうかんごに　きこくします。

▶ **Altogether, I will be in Japan for three weeks.**
  Zenbu-de san-shū-kan Nihon-ni imasu.
  (Zem-boo day sahn-shuu-kahn nee-hoan nee ee-mahss)
  ぜんぶで　さんしゅうかん　にほんに　います。

▶ **Can you extend my reservations for one more week?**
  Yoyaku-o ato is-shū-kan nobasemasen-ka.
  (Yoe-yah-kuu oh ah-toe ish-shuu-kahn no-bah-say mah-sen kah)
  よやくを　あと　いっしゅうかん　のばせませんか。

THE MONTHS

Japanese for month is **gatsu** (got-sue) がつ when used in a general sense, and **getsu** (get-sue) げつ when expressing month-long periods of time. To name the months of the year, just add the Chinese set of numbers one through twelve:

January	*ichi-gatsu (ee-chee-got-sue)*	いちがつ
February	*ni-gatsu (nee-got-sue)*	にがつ
March	*san-gatsu (sahn-got-sue)*	さんがつ
April	*shi-gatsu (she-got-sue)*	しがつ
May	*go-gatsu (go-got-sue)*	ごがつ
June	*roku-gatsu (roe-kuu-got-sue)*	ろくがつ
July	*shichi-gatsu (she-chee-got-sue)*	しちがつ
August	*hachi-gatsu (hah-chee-got-sue)*	はちがつ
September	*ku-gatsu (kuu-got-sue)*	くがつ
October	*jū-gatsu (juu-got-sue)*	じゅうがつ
November	*jū-ichi-gatsu*	じゅういちがつ
	(juu-ee-chee-got-sue)	
December	*jū-ni-gatsu*	じゅうにがつ
	(juu-nee-got-sue)	
month before last	*sensengetsu (sen sen get-sue)*	せんせんげつ
last month	*sengetsu (sen get-sue)*	せんげつ
this month	*kongetsu (kone get-sue)*	こんげつ
next month	*raigetsu (rye get-sue)*	らいげつ
month after next	*saraigetsu (sah rye get-sue)*	さらいげつ
every month	*maitsuki (my t'sue-kee)*	まいつき

▶ **I will return this month.**
Kongetsu modorimasu.
(Kone get-sue moe-doe-ree-mahss)
こんげつ　もどります。

▶ **Will the weather get better next month?**
Raigetsu-ni-wa tenki-ga yoku narimasu-ka.
(Rye get-sue nee wah ten-kee gah yoe-kuu nah-ree-mahss kah)
らいげつには　てんきが　よく　なりますか。

▶ **My birthday was last month.**
Watashi-no tanjōbi-wa sengetsu-deshita.
(Wah-tah-she no tahn-joe-bee wah sen get-sue desh-tah)
わたしの　たんじょうびは　せんげつでした。

▶ **Does it rain often in June in Japan?**
Nihon-de-wa roku-gatsu-ni yoku ame-ga furimasu-ka.
(Nee-hoan day wah roe-kuu-got-sue nee yoe-kuu ah-may gah who-ree-mahss kah)
にほんでは　ろくがつに　よく　あめが　ふりますか。

▶ **Will it get hot in August?**
Hachi-gatsu-wa atsuku narimasu-ka.
(Hah-chee-got-sue wah aht-sue-kuu nah-ree-mahss kah)
はちがつは　あつく　なりますか。

▶ **I am going to be in the Tokyo branch from April to September.**
Watashi-wa shi-gatsu-kara ku-gatsu-made Tōkyō-shisha-ni imasu.
(Wa-tah-she wah she-got-sue kah-rah kuu-got-sue mah-day toe-k'yoe she-shah nee ee-mahss)
わたしは　しがつから　くがつまで　とうきょうししゃに　います。

COUNTING MONTHS

Months are counted by combining the numeral and *ka-getsu* (kah-get-sue) かげつ.

one month	*ik-ka-getsu* いっかげつ
	(eek-kah-get-sue)
two months	*ni-ka-getsu* にかげつ
	(nee-kah-get-sue)
three months	*san-ka-getsu* さんかげつ
	(sahn-kah-get-sue)
four months	*yon-ka-getsu* よんかげつ
	(yoan-kah-get-sue)
five months	*go-ka-getsu* ごかげつ
	(go-kah-get-sue)
six month	*rok-ka-getsu* ろっかげつ
	(roak-kah-get-sue)
seven months	*nana-ka-getsu* ななかげつ
	(nah-nah-kah-get-sue)
eight months	*hachi-ka-getsu* はちかげつ
	(hah-chee-kah-get-sue)
nine months	*kyū-ka-getsu* きゅうかげつ
	(queue-kah-get-sue)
ten months	*juk-ka-getsu* じゅっかげつ
	(juuk-kah-get-sue)
eleven months	*jū-ik-ka-getsu* じゅういっかげつ
	(juu-eek-kah-get-sue)
twelve months	*jū-ni-ka-getsu* じゅうにかげつ
	(juu-nee-kah-get-sue)
a few months	*sū-ka-getsu* すうかげつ
	(sue-kah-get-sue)

▶ **How many months are you going to be here?**
Nan-ka-getsu-gurai koko-ni imasu-ka.
(Nahn kah-get-sue guu-rye koe-koe nee ee-mahss kah)
なんかげつぐらい　ここに　いますか。

▶ **I am going to be in Japan for five months.**
Go-ka-getsu Nihon-ni imasu.
(Go-kah-get-sue nee-hoan nee ee-mahss)
ごかげつ　にほんに　います。

▶ **This project will take two months.**
Kono-purojekuto-wa ni-ka-getsu kakarimasu.
(Koe-no puu-roe-jey-kuu-toe wah nee kah get-sue kah-kah-ree-mahss)
このプロジェクトは　にかげつ　かかります。

GIVING DATES

A special word, *tsuitachi (t'sue-ee-tah-chee)* ついたち, is used for the 1st or "first" day of the month. For example, April 1st is **shi-gatsu tsuitachi** *(she-got-sue t'sue-ee-tah-chee)* しがつ ついたち. From the 2nd onwards, the terms introduced in "Counting Days" are used for giving dates as well.

1st *tsuitachi (t'sue-ee-tah-chee)* ついたち
2nd *futsu-ka (who-t'sue-kah)* ふつか
3rd *mik-ka (meek-kah)* みっか
4th *yok-ka (yoke-kah)* よっか
5th *itsu-ka (ee-t'sue-kah)* いつか
6th *mui-ka (muu-ee-kah)* むいか
7th *nano-ka (nah-no-kah)* なのか
8th *yō-ka (yoh-kah)* ようか
9th *kokono-ka (koe-koe-no-kah)* ここのか
10th *tō-ka (toh-kah)* とおか
11th *jū-ichi-nichi* じゅういちにち
　　　(juu-ee-chee-nee-chee)

12th *jū-ni-nichi (juu-nee-nee-chee)* じゅうににち
13th *jū-san-nichi* じゅうさんにち
         (juu-sahn-nee-chee)
14th *jū-yok-ka (juu-yoke-kah)* じゅうよっか
15th *jū-go-nichi (juu-go-nee-chee)* じゅうごにち
18th *jū-hachi-nichi* じゅうはちにち
         (juu-hah-chee nee-chee)
20th *hatsu-ka (hah-t'sue-kah)* はつか
21st *ni-jū-ichi-nichi* にじゅういちにち
         (nee-juu-ee-chee-nee-chee)
24th *ni-jū-yok-ka (nee-juu-yoke-kah)* にじゅうよっか
26th *ni-jū-roku-nichi* にじゅうろくにち
         (nee-juu-roe-kuu-nee-chee)
30th *san-jū-nichi (sahn-juu-nee-chee)* さんじゅうにち

▶ **What day of the month is today?**
   Kyō-wa nan-nichi-desu-ka. きょうは　なんにちですか。
   (K'yoe wah nahn-nee-chee dess kah)

▶ **It's the 5th.**
   Itsuka-desu. (Ee-t'sue-kah dess) いつかです。

▶ **Tomorrow will be the 6th.**
   Ashita-wa mui-ka-desu. あしたは　むいかです。
   (Ah-ssh-tah wah muu-ee-kah dess)

▶ **Today is November 28th.**
   Kyō-wa jū-ichi-gatsu ni-jū-hachi-nichi-desu.
   (K'yoe wah juu-ee-chee-got-sue nee-juu-hah-chee-nee-chee dess)
   きょうは　じゅういちがつ　にじゅうはちにちです。

▶ **We are going to Osaka on the 21st.**
Ni-jū-ichi-nichi-ni Ōsaka-ni ikimasu.
(Nee-juu-ee-chee-nee-chee nee oh-sah-kah nee ee-kee-mahss)
にじゅういちにちに　おおさかに　いきます。

▶ **We will leave (for our country) on the 18th.**
Jū-hachi-nichi-ni kaerimasu.
(Juu-hah-chee nee-chee nee kah-eh-ree-mahss)
じゅうはちにちに　かえります。

▶ **I am going to Japan on June 10th.**
Roku-gatsu tō-ka-ni Nihon-ni ikimasu.
(Roe-kuu-got-sue toh-kah nee nee-hoan nee ee-kee-mahss)
ろくがつ　とおかに　にほんに　いきます。

▶ **Please respond/reply by July 15th.**
Shichi-gatsu jū-go-nichi-made-ni o-henji kudasai.
(She-chee-got-sue juu-go-nee-chee mah-day nee ohen-jee kuu-dah-sie)
しちがつ　じゅうごにちまでに　おへんじ　ください。

THE YEARS

year	*toshi (toe-she)* とし or *nen (nen)* ねん
year before last	*issakunen* いっさくねん *(ees-sah-kuu nen)*
last year	*kyonen (k'yoe nen)* きょねん or *sakunen (sah-kuu nen)* さくねん
this year	*kotoshi (koe toe-she)* ことし
next year	*rainen (rye nen)* らいねん

year after next	*sarainen (sah-rye nen)* さらいねん
every year	*maitoshi (my toe-she)* まいとし or
	mainen (my nen) まいねん
new year	*shinnen (sheen nen)* しんねん
year round	*ichi-nen-jū (ee-chee nen-juu)* いちねんじゅう
new year's eve	*ōmisoka* おおみそか *(oh-me-soh-kah)*
new year's day	*ganjitsu (ghan jeet-sue)* がんじつ
for half a year	*han-toshi (hahn toe-she)* はんとし or **han-toshi-kan** はんとしかん *(hahn toe-she kahn)*
for one year	*ichi-nen (ee-chee nen)* いちねん or *ichi-nen-kan* いちねんかん *(ee-chee nen kahn)*
for one and a half years	*ichi-nen-han (ee-chee nen hahn)* いちねんはん
for two years	*ni-nen (nee nen)* にねん or *ni-nen-kan* にねんかん *(nee nen kahn)*
for three years	*san-nen (sahn nen)* さんねん or *san-nen-kan (sahn nen kahn)* さんねんかん

▶ **I have studied Japanese for one year.**
  Ichi-nen-kan Nihon-go-o benkyō-shimashita.
  (Ee-chee nen kahn nee-hoan-go oh bane-k'yoe she-mah-sshtah)
  いちねんかん　にほんごを　べんきょうしました。

▶ **I came to Japan this January.**
  Kotoshi-no ichi-gatsu-ni Nihon-ni kimashita.
  (Koe toe-she no ee-chee-got-sue nee nee-hoan nee kee-mah-sshtah)
  ことしの　いちがつに　にほんに　きました。

▶ **I will stay here until next August.**
  Rainen-no hachi-gatsu-made koko-ni imasu.
  (Rye nen no hah-chee-got-sue mah-day koe-koe nee ee-mahss)
  らいねんの　はちがつまで　ここに　います。

▶ **A Happy New Year!**
  Akemashite omedetō gozaimasu.
  (Ah-kay-mah-she-tay oh-may-day-toe go-zie-mahss)
  あけまして　おめでとう　ございます。

Note that this expression is used only after a new year has come.

Japan now uses two systems for counting years, the Western system and their own traditional system of figuring years on the basis of the reign of the current emperor. The reign of each emperor is given a name, such as *Meiji (may-jee)* めいじ, *Shōwa (show-wah)* しょうわ and *Heisei (hay-say)* へいせい, and thereafter years are counted as *Heisei ni-jū-nen (hay-say nee-juu-nen)* へいせい　にじゅうねん "the 20th year of Heisei." Nowadays younger people are more familiar with the Western system of counting the years than older people.

1990 *sen-kyū-hyaku-kyū-jū-nen*
(*sen queue-h'yah-kuu queue-juu nen*)
せん　きゅうひゃく　きゅうじゅうねん or,
Heisei ni-nen (*hay-say nee nen*)
へいせい　にねん "the 2nd year of Heisei"

1995 *sen-kyū-hyaku-kyū-jū-go-nen*
(*sen queue-h'yah-kuu queue-juu-go nen*)
せん　きゅうひゃく　じゅうごねん

2000 *ni-sen-nen* (*nee-sen nen*) にせんねん

2005 *ni-sen-go-nen* (*nee-sen go nen*) にせん　ごねん

2010 *ni-sen-jū-nen* (*nee-sen juu nen*)
にせん　じゅうねん or,
Heisei ni-jū-ni-nen (*hay-say nee nen*)
へいせい　にじゅうにねん "the 22nd year of Heisei"

▶ **I was born in 1970.**
   Watashi-wa sen-kyū-hyaku-nana-jū-nen-ni umare-
   mashita.
   (*Wah-tah-she wah sen queue h'yah-kuu nah-nah juu nen*
   nee uu-mah-ray-mah-sshtah)
   わたしは　せん　きゅうひゃく　ななじゅうねんに
   うまれ　ました。

▶ **I have been working for this company since April 1993.**
   Sen-kyū-hyaku-kyū-jū-san-nen-no shigatsu-kara kono
   kaisha-ni tsutomete imasu.
   (*Sen queue-h'yah-kuu queue-juu-shan nen no she-got-sue*
   kah-rah koe-no kie-shah nee t'sue-toe-may-tay ee-mahss)
   せん　きゅうひゃく　きゅうじゅうさんねんの　しがつから
   この　かいしゃに　つとめて　います。

THE SEASONS

season	*kisetsu (kee-set-sue)*	きせつ
spring	*haru (hah-rue)*	はる
summer	*natsu (not-sue)*	なつ
fall	*aki (ah-kee)*	あき
winter	*fuyu (who-yuu)*	ふゆ

▶ **When does spring start?**
   Itsu-goro haru-ni narimasu-ka.
   (Eet-sue go-roe hah-rue nee nah-ree-mahss kah)
   いつごろ　はるに　なりますか。

▶ **The weather is fine in the fall.**
   Aki-wa tenki-ga ii-desu. あきは　てんきが　いいです。
   (Ah-kee wah ten-kee gah ee dess)

▶ **I like summer the best.**
   Watashi-wa natsu-ga ichiban suki-desu.
   (Wah-tah-she wah not-sue gah ee-chee-bahn sue-kee dess)
   わたしは　なつが　いちばん　すきです。

THE TIME

In Japanese "minute" is *fun (whoon)* ふん or *pun (poon)* ぷ
ん, time in a generic sense (o'clock) is *ji (jee)* じ, and the duration of time (or "hour") is *ji (jee)* じ plus *kan (kahn)* かん or
ji-kan (jee-kahn) じかん. These terms combined with numbers
of the Chinese set give us the time. There are slight euphonic
changes in the spellings to accommodate pronunciation.

time	*jikan (jee-kahn)* じかん
one minute	*ip-pun (eep-poon)* いっぷん
two minutes	*ni-fun (nee-whoon)* にふん
three minutes	*san-pun (sahn-poon)* さんぷん
four minutes	*yon-pun (yone-poon)* よんぷん
five minutes	*go-fun (go-whoon)* ごふん
six minutes	*rop-pun (rope-poon)* ろっぷん
seven minutes	*nana-fun (nah-nah-whoon)* ななふん
eight minutes	*hap-pun (hop-poon)* はっぷん
nine minutes	*kyū-fun (queue-whoon)* きゅうふん
ten minutes	*jup-pun (juup-poon)* じゅっぷん
eleven minutes	*jū-ip-pun* じゅういっぷん *(juu-eep-poon)*
twelve minutes	*jū-ni-fun* じゅうにふん *(juu-nee-whoon)*
fifteen minutes	*jū-go-fun* じゅうごふん *(juu-go-whoon)*
twenty minutes	*ni-jup-pun* にじゅっぷん *(nee-juup-poon)*
thirty minutes	*san-jup-pun* さんじゅっぷん *(sahn-juup-poon)*
forty minutes	*yon-jup-pun (yone-juup-poon)* よんじゅっぷん
fifty minutes	*go-jup-pun* ごじゅっぷん *(go-juup-poon)*
one hour	*ichi-ji-kan* いちじかん *(ee-chee jee-kahn)*
two hours	*ni-ji-kan (nee jee-kahn)* にじかん
three hours	*san-ji-kan* さんじかん *(sahn jee-kahn)*
four hours	*yo-ji-kan (yoe jee-kahn)* よじかん
five hours	*go-ji-kan (go jee-kahn)* ごじかん

six hours	*roku-ji-kan* ろくじかん
	(roe-kuu jee-kahn)
seven hours	*nana-ji-kan* ななじかん
	(nah-nah jee-kahn) or
	shichi-ji-kan しちじかん
	(she-chee jee-kahn)
eight hours	*hachi-ji-kan* はちじかん
	(hah-chee jee-kahn)
nine hours	*ku-ji-kan (kuu jee-kahn)* くじかん
ten hours	*jū-ji-kan* じゅうじかん
	(juu jee-kahn)
eleven hours	*jū-ichi-ji-kan* じゅういちじかん
	(juu-ee-chee jee-kahn)
twelve hours	*jū-ni-ji-kan* じゅうにじかん
	(juu-nee jee-kahn)
half an hour	*sun-jup-pun* さんじゅっぷん
	(sahn-juup-poon)
one and a half hours	*ichi-ji-kan san-jup-pun*
	(ee-chee jee-kahn sahn-juup-poon)
	いちじかん さんじゅっぷん or
	ichi-ji-kan-han いちじかんはん
	(ee-chee jee-kahn hahn)
noon	*shōgo (show-go)* しょうご
midnight	*mayonaka* まよなか
	(mah-yoe-nah-kah)
1 o'clock	*ichi-ji (ee-chee-jee)* いちじ
1 p.m.	*gogo ichi-ji* ごご　いちじ
	(go-go ee-chee-jee)
1 a.m.	*gozen ichi-ji* ごぜん　いちじ
	(go-zen ee-chee-jee)
1:15	*ichi-ji jū-go-fun* いちじ　じゅうごふん
	(ee-chee-jee juu-go-whoon)

1:30	*ichi-ji san-jup-pun* いちじ　さんじゅっぷん
	(ee-che-jee sahn-juup-poon) or
	ichi-ji han (ee-chee-jee hahn) いちじ　はん
1:45	*ichi-ji yon-jū-go-fun*
	(ee-chee-jee yoan-juu-go-whoon)
	いちじ　よんじゅうごふん
2 o'clock	*ni-ji (nee-jee)* にじ
3 o'clock	*san-ji (sahn-jee)* さんじ
10 to 3	*san-ji jup-pun-mae* さんじ　じゅっぷんまえ
	(sahn-jee juup-poon mah-eh)
5 to 4	*yo-ji go-fun-mae* よじ　ごふんまえ
	(yoe-jee go-whoon mah-eh)

► **What time is it now?**
  Ima nan-ji-desu-ka. いま　なんじですか。
  (Ee-mah nahn-jee dess kah)

► **It's 4:25.**
  Yo-ji ni-jū-go-fun-desu. よじ　にじゅうごふんです。
  (Yoe-jee nee-juu-go-whoon dess)

get up/ wake up	*okimasu (oh-kee-mahss)* おきます
departure	*shuppatsu (shupe-pot-sue)* しゅっぱつ
breakfast	*asa-gohan (ah-sah-go-hahn)* あさごはん
	or *chōshoku* ちょうしょく
	(choe-show-kuu)
lunch	*hiru-gohan (he-rue-go-hahn)* ひるごはん
	or *chūshoku* ちゅうしょく
	(chuu-show-kuu)
dinner	*ban-gohan (bahn-go-hahn)* ばんごはん
	or *yūshoku (yuu-show-kuu)* ゆうしょく

▶ **What time shall I/we get up?**
Nan-ji-ni okimashō-ka. なんじに　おきましょうか。
(Nahn-jee nee oh-kee-mah-show kah)

▶ **What time does breakfast begin?**
Chōshoku-wa nan-ji-kara-desu-ka.
(Choe-show-kuu wah nahn-jee kah-rah dess kah)
ちょうしょくは　なんじからですか。

▶ **Breakfast begins at 7 o'clock.**
Chōshoku-wa shichi-ji-kara-desu.
(Choe-show-kuu wah she-chee jee kah-rah dess)
ちょうしょくは　しちじからです。

▶ **What time is lunch?**
Chūshoku-wa nan-ji-desu-ka.
(Chuu-show-kuu wah nahn-jee dess kah)
ちゅうしょくは　なんじですか。

▶ **Lunch will be between noon and 1 o'clock.**
Chūshoku-wa shōgo-kara ichi-ji-made-desu.
(Chuu-show-kuu wah show-go kah-rah ee-chee-jee mah-day dess)
ちゅうしょくは　しょうごから　いちじまでです。

▶ **What time shall we have dinner?**
Yūshoku-wa nan-ji-ni shimashō-ka.
(Yuu-show-kuu wah nahn-jee nee she-mah-show kah)
ゆうしょくは　なんじに　しましょうか。

▶ Let's make it at 6:30.
  Roku-ji-han-ni shimashō. ろくじはんじに　しましょう。
  (Roe-kuu-jee hahn nee she-mah-show)

▶ What time are we going out?
  Nan-ji-ni dekakemasu-ka. なんじに　でかけますか。
  (Nahn-jee nee day-kah-kay mahss kah)

▶ We'll leave at 8:15.
  Hachi-ji jū-go-fun-ni demasu.
  (Hah-chee-jee juu-go-whoon nee day-mahss)
  はちじ　じゅうごふんに　でます。

▶ What time is the bus leaving?
  Basu-wa nan-ji-ni demasu-ka.
  (Bah-sue wah nahn-jee nee day-mahss kah)
  バスは　なんじに　でますか。

▶ What time does the meeting start?
  Kaigi-wa nan-ji-ni hajimarimasu-ka.
  (Kie-ghee wah nahn-jee nee hah-jee-mah-ree-mahss kah)
  かいぎは　なんじに　はじまりますか。

▶ It starts at 3:30.
  San-ji-han-kara-desu. さんじはんからです。
  (Sahn-jee hahn kah-rah dess)

▶ What time do department stores open?
  Depāto-wa nan-ji-ni akimasu-ka.
  (Day-paah-toe wah nahn-jee nee ah-kee-mahss kah)
  デパートは　なんじに　あきますか。

▶ **What time is your departure?**
Shuppatsu-wa nan-ji-desu-ka.
(Shupe-pot-sue wah nahn-jee dess kah)
しゅっぱつは　なんじですか。

▶ **It's 10 to 9.**
Ku-ji jup-pun-mae-desu. くじ　じゅっぷんまえです。
(Kuu-jee juup-poon mah-eh dess)

▶ **What time is the appointment?**
Yakusoku-wa nan-ji-desu-ka.
(Yahk-soe-kuu wah nahn-jee dess kah)
やくそくは　なんじですか。

▶ **Will this take very much time?**
Kore-wa zuibun jikan-ga kakarimasu-ka.
(Koe-ray wah zoo-ee-boon jee-kahn gah kah-kah-ree-mahss kah)
これは　ずいぶん　じかんが　かかりますか。

▶ **I think it will take about five hours.**
Go-ji-kan-gurai kakaru-to omoimasu.
(Go jee-kahn guu-rye kah-kah-rue-toe oh-moy-ee-mahss)
ごじかんぐらい　かかると　おもいます。

▶ **Is that place close to the hotel?**
Soko-wa hoteru-kara chikai-desu-ka.
(So-koe wah hoe-tay-rue kah-rah chee-kie dess kah)
そこは　ホテルから　ちかいですか。

▶ **I think it is about 5 minutes on foot.**
Aruite go-fun-gurai-da-to omoimasu.
(*Ah-rue-ee-tay go-whoon guu-rye dah-toe oh-moy-ee-mahss*)
あるいて　ごふんぐらい　だと　おもいます。

▶ **Will we go now?**
Mō dekakemasu-ka. もう　でかけますか。
(*Moe day-kah-kay-mahss kah*)

▶ **I/We still have plenty of time.**
Mada jūbun jikan-ga arimasu.
(*Mah-dah juu-boon jee-kahn gah ah-ree-mahss*)
まだ　じゅうぶん　じかんが　あります。

▶ **I/We have no more time.**
Mō jikan-ga arimasen. もう　じかんが　ありません。
(*Moe jee-kahn gah ah-ree-mah-sen*)

▶ **I'll be back in a short time.**
Sugu modotte kimasu. すぐ　もどって　きます。
(*Sue-goo moe-doet-tay kee-mahss*)

▶ **I'll be back in 10 minutes.**
Jup-pun-de modotte kimasu.
(*Juup-poon day moe-doet-tay kee-mahss*)
じゅっぷんで　もどって　きます。

▶ **I'll do it within an hour.**
Ichi-ji-kan-de shimasu. いちじかんで　します。
(*Ee-chee jee-kahn day she-mahss*)

leisure time	*hima (he-mah)* ひま
early	*hayai (hah-yie)* はやい
late	*osoi (oh-soy)* おそい
on time	*jikan-dōri* じかんどおり *(jee-kahn doe-ree)*
be late (for ...)	*(... ni) okuremasu* ……に おくれます。 *((...nee) oh-kuu-ray mahss)*
be on time	*maniaimasu* まにあいます。 *(mah-nee-ah-ee-mahss)*
if	*ta*-form (i.e. plain past affirmative form) + *ra (rah)* ら

▶ **Are you free now?**
Ima hima-ga arimasu-ka.
(Ee-mah he-mah gah ah-ree-mass kah?)
いま　ひまが　ありますか。
Ima jikan-ga arimasu-ka.
(Ee-mah jee-kahn gah ah-ree-mass kah)
いま　じかんが　ありますか。

▶ **Yes, I am (free).**
Ee, arimasu. (Eeh, ah-ree-mahss) ええ、あります。

▶ **Oh, I am afraid not now.**
Ā, ima-wa chotto. あー、いまは　ちょっと。
(Ah, ee-mah wah choat-toe)

▶ **If you are free this evening, would you like to go for a drink with me?**
Konban hima-datta-ra, issho-ni nomi-ni ikimasen-ka.
(*Kome-bahn he-mah-dat-tah-rah, ish-show nee no-me nee ee-kee-mah-sen kah*)
こんばん　ひまだったら、いっしょに　のみに
いきませんか。

▶ **If I have time, I would like to go to Akihabara.**
Jikan-ga atta-ra, akihabara-ni ikitai-desu.
(*Jee-kahn gah at-tah-rah aah-kee-hah-bah-rah nee ee-kee-tie dess*)
じかんが　あったら、あきはばらに　いきたいです。

▶ **It is late, isn't it. / He/She is late, isn't he/she.**
Osoi-desu-ne. (*Oh-soy dess nay*) おそいですね。

Note that *ne* (*nay*) ね is used at the end of a sentence to ask the listener for agreement/confirmation and is equivalent to the tag question (e.g. isn't it) in English.

▶ **It is still early.**
Mada hayai-desu. まだ　はやいです。
(*Mah-dah hah-yie dess*)

▶ **We/you are going to be late for the meeting.**
Kaigi-ni okuremasu-yo. かいぎに　おくれますよ。
(*Kie-ghee nee oh-kuu-ray mahss yoe*)

Note that *yo* (*yoe*) よ is used at the end of a sentence to express one's opinion strongly and is equivalent to "I tell you" or "you know."

▶ **We are on time.**
Jikan dōri desu. じかん　どおりです。
(Jee-kahn dore-ree dess)

▶ **If we/you hurry, we/you can still get there on time.**
Isoida-ra, mada maniaimasu-yo.
(Ee-soy-dah-rah, mah-dah mah-nee-ah-ee-mahss yoe)
いそいだら、まだ　まにあいますよ。

THE WEATHER

weather	*tenki (ten-kee)* てんき or *tenkō (ten-koe)* てんこう
weather forecast	*tenki-yohō* てんきよほう *(ten-kee yoe-hoe)*
hot	*atsui (aht-sue-ee)* あつい
hot and humid	*mushiatsui* むしあつい *(muu-she aht-sue-ee)*
warm	*atatakai (aht-tah-tah-kie)* あたたかい
cool	*suzushii (sue-zoo-she)* すずしい
cold	*samui (sah-muu-ee)* さむい
fine weather	*hare (hah-ray)* はれ
cloudy weather	*kumori (kuu-moe-ree)* くもり
wind	*kaze (kah-zay)* かぜ
rain	*ame (ah-may)* あめ
snow	*yuki (yuu-kee)* ゆき
good	*ii (ee-ee)* いい
bad	*warui (wah-rue-ee)* わるい
strong	*tsuyoi (t'sue-yoe-ee)* つよい
umbrella	*kasa (kah-sah)* かさ

▶ **It's a nice day, isn't it.**
Ii o-tenki-desu-ne. いい　おてんきですね。
(Ee-ee oh-ten-kee dess nay)

▶ **It's hot, isn't it.**
Atsui-desu-ne. *(Aht-sue-ee dess nay)* あついですね。

▶ **It's cold, isn't it.**
Samui-desu-ne. *(Sah-muu-ee dess nay)* さむいですね。

▶ **Will it rain tonight?**
Kon'ya-wa ame-ga furimasu-ka.
(Kone-yah wah ah-may gah who-ree-mahss kah)
こんやは　あめが　ふりますか。

▶ **According to the weather forecast, it will rain.**
Tenki-yohō-ni-yoru-to, ame-ga furu sō-desu.
(Ten-kee yoe-hoe nee yoe-rue-toe ah-may gah who-rue so-dess)
てんきよほうによると、　あめが　ふる　そうです。

▶ **How will the weather be tomorrow?**
Ashita-no tenki-wa dō-desu-ka.
(Ah-ssh-tah no ten-kee wah doh dess kah)
あしたの　てんきは　どうですか。

▶ **According to the weather forecast, it will be fine.**
Tenki-yohō-ni-yoru-to, hare-da sō-desu.
(Ten-kee yoe-hoe nee yoe-rue-toe hah-ray-dah so-dess)
てんきよほうによると、　はれだ　そうです。

▶ **It is raining.**
Ame-ga futte imasu. あめが　ふって　います。
(Ah-may gah whoot-tay ee-mahss)

▶ **It is snowing.**
Yuki-ga futte imasu. ゆきが　ふって　います。
(Yuu-kee gah whoot-tay ee-mahss)

▶ **It is windy.**
Kaze-ga tsuyoi-desu. かぜが　つよいです。
(Kah-zay gah t'sue-yoe-ee dess)

▶ **It looks like it will rain today, doesn't it.**
Kyō-wa ame-ga furi-sō-desu-ne.
(K'yoe wah ah-may gah who-ree-so dess nay)
きょうは　あめが　ふりそうですね。

▶ **It will probably clear up by this afternoon.**
Gogo-made-ni hareru-deshō.
(Go-go mah-day nee hah-ray-rue day-show)
ごごまでに　はれるでしょう。

▶ **Do I need an umbrella?**
Kasa-ga irimasu-ka. かさが　いりますか。
(Kah-sah gah ee-ree-mass kah)

USING MONEY

money	*o-kane* (oh-kah-nay) おかね
yen	*en* (ehn) えん
dollar(s)	*doru* (doe-rue) ドル

exchange rate	*kōkan-rēto* こうかんレート
	(koe-kahn ray-toe)
change	*o-tsuri (oh-t'sue-ree)* おつり
small change	*kozeni (koe-zay-nee)* こぜに
break a bill	*komakaku-suru* こまかくする
	(koe-mah-kah-kuu sue-rue)
expensive	*takai (tah-kie)* たかい
cheap	*yasui (yah-sue-ee)* やすい
how much	*ikura (ee-kuu-rah)* いくら
budget	*yosan (yoe-sahn)* よさん

► **What is today's exchange rate?**
Kyō-no kōkan-rēto-wa ikura-desu-ka.
(K'yoe no koe-kahn ray-toe wah ee-kuu-rah dess kah)
きょうの　こうかんレートは　いくらですか。

► **Would you please change $100 into yen?**
Hyaku-doru-o en-ni kōkan-shite moraemasen-ka.
(H'yah-kuu doe-rue oh ehn nee koe-kahn she-tay-moe-rah-eh-mah-sen kah)
ひゃくドルを　えんに　こうかんして　もらえませんか。

► **How much is this in dollars?**
Kore-wa doru-de ikura-desu-ka.
(Koe-ray wah doe-rue day ee-kuu-rah dess kah)
これは　ドルで　いくらですか。

► **Would you please break this (into coins)?**
Kore-o komakaku-shite moraemasen-ka.
(Koe-ray oh koe-mah-kah-kuu ssh-tay moe-rah-eh-mah-sen kah)
これを　こまかくして　もらえませんか。

▶ **Do you have any Japanese yen?**
Nihon-en-wa arimasen-ka. にほんえんは　ありませんか。
(Nee-hoan ehn wah ah-ree-mah-sen kah)

▶ **My budget is 30,000 yen.**
Yosan-wa san-man-en-desu.
(Yoe-sahn wah sahm-mahn ehn dess)
よさんは　さんまんえんです。

▶ **This is a little too expensive.**
Kore-wa chotto takai-desu-ne.
(Koe-ray wah choat-toe tah-kie dess nay)
これは　ちょっと　たかいですね。

▶ **Do you have a little cheaper ones?**
Mō sukoshi yasui-no-wa arimasen-ka.
(Moe sue-koe-she yah-sue-ee no wah ah-ree-mah-sen kah)
もう　すこし　やすいのは　ありませんか。

▶ **Can you make it a little cheaper?**
Mō sukoshi yasuku narimasen-ka.
(Moe sue-koe-she yah-sue-koo nah-ree-mah-sen kah)
もう　すこし　やすく　なりませんか。

IN A RESTAURANT

menu	*menyū (men-yuu)* メニュー
English menu	*eigo-no menyū* えいごの　メニュー
	(aa-go no men-yuu)
counter	*kauntā (kah-uun-tah)* カウンター
table	*tēburu (tay-buu-rue)* テーブル

chair	*isu* (ee-sue) いす
Japanese-style room	*zashiki* (zah-she-kee) ざしき or *washitsu* (wah-she-t'sue) わしつ
cushion	*zabuton* (zah-boo-ton) ざぶとん
share-seat (table)	*ai-seki* (aye-say-kee) あいせき
grill cooking	*teppan-yaki* てっぱんやき (tep-pahn yah-kee)
deep-fried foods	*age-mono* あげもの (ah-gay moe-no)
pot dishes	*nabe-mono* なべもの (nah-bay moe-no)
broiled dishes	*yaki-mono* やきもの (yah-kee moe-no)
rice with toppings	*donburi-mono* どんぶりもの (dome-buu-ree moe-no)
set meal	*teishoku* ていしょく (tay-show-kuu)
side dishes	*sōzai* (soe zie) そうざい
boxed food	*bentō* (ben-toe) べんとう
take out food	*mochi-kaeri* もちかえり (moe-chee kah-eh-ree)
food delivery	*demae* (day-mah-eh) でまえ
serving for one	*ichi-nin-mae* いちにんまえ (ee-chee-neen mah-eh)
serving for two	*ni-nin-mae* ににんまえ (nee-neen mah-eh)
serving for three	*san-nin-mae* さんにんまえ (sahn-neen mah-eh)
bread	*pan* (pahn) パン
rice (in a bowl)	*gohan* (go-hahn) ごはん

rice (on a plate)	*raisu (rye-sue)* ライス
soup	*sūpu (sue-puu)* スープ
miso soup	*miso-shiru* みそしる *(me-so-she-rue)*
steak	*sutēki (suu-tay-kee)* ステーキ
well-done	*weru-dan (way-rue dahn)* ウェルダン
medium	*midiamu (me-dee-ahm)* ミディアム
rare	*rea (ray-ah)* レア
beef	*bīfu (bee-who)* ビーフ
chicken	*chikin (chee-keen)* チキン
pork	*pōku (poh-kuu)* ポーク
fish	*sakana (sah-kah-nah)* さかな
dessert	*dezāto (day-zah-toe)* デザート
ice cream	*aisukurīmu* アイスクリーム *(aye-sue kuu-ree-muu)*
cake	*kēki (kay-kee)* ケーキ
fruit	*furūtsu (who-rue-t'sue)* フルーツ or *kudamono (kuu-dah-moe-no)* くだもの
salt	*shio (she-oh)* しお
pepper	*koshō (koe-show)* こしょう
sugar	*satō (sah-toe)* さとう
soy sauce	*shōyu (show-yuu)* しょうゆ
regular sauce	*sōsu (soe-suu)* ソース
coffee	*kōhī (koe-hee)* コーヒー
brown (black) **tea**	*kōcha (koe-chah)* こうちゃ
green tea	*o-cha (oh-chah)* おちゃ or *ban-cha (bahn chah)* ばんちゃ
cream	*kurīmu (kuu-ree-muu)* クリーム
milk	*miruku (me-rue-kuu)* ミルク
water	*mizu (me-zuu)* みず

hot water	*o-yu (oh-yuu)* おゆ
orange juice	*orenji-jūsu* オレンジジュース *(oh-rane-jee juu-suu)*
tomato juice	*tomato jūsu* トマトジュース *(toe-mah-toe juu-suu)*
cola	*kōra (koe-rah)* コーラ
knife	*naifu (nie-who)* ナイフ
fork	*fōku (foh-kuu)* フォーク
spoon	*supūn (sue-poon)* スプーン
chopsticks	*hashi (hah-shee)* はし
toothpick	*tsumayōji* つまようじ *(t'sue-mah yoe-jee)*
drinking glass	*koppu (kope-puu)* コップ or *gurasu (goo-rah-sue)* グラス
napkin	*napukin (nah-puu-keen)* ナプキン
wet towel	*oshibori (oh-she-boe-ree)* おしぼり
delicious	*oishii (oh-ee-shee)* おいしい
not delicious	*mazui (mah-zuu-ee)* まずい
sweet	*amai (ah-my)* あまい
spicy hot	*karai (kah-rye)* からい
salty	*shio-karai (she-oh kah-rye)* しおからい
hot	*atsui (aht-sue-ee)* あつい
cold (to the touch)	*tsumetai (t'sue-may-tie)* つめたい

▶ **I'm hungry.**
Onaka-ga sukimashita. おなかが　すきました。
(Oh-nah-ka gah sue-kee-mah-sshtah)

▶ **I'm thirsty.**
Nodo-ga kawakimashita. のどが　かわきました。
(No-doe gah kah-wah-kee-mah-sshtah)

▶ **Why don't we have a meal?**
Shokuji-ni shimasen-ka. しょくじに　しませんか。
(Show-kuu-jee nee she-mah-sen kah)

▶ **Let's take a rest at a coffee shop.**
Chotto kissa-ten-de yasumimashō.
(Choat-toe kees-sah-ten day yah-sue-me-mah-show)
ちょっと　きっさてんで　やすみましょう。

▶ **Welcome! How many people?**
Irasshaimase. Nan-mei-sama-desu-ka.
(Ee-rash-shy-mah-say. Nahn-may-sah-mah dess kah)
いらっしゃいませ。なんめいさまですか。

▶ **Just the two of us.**
Futari-desu. (Who-tah-ree dess) ふたりです。

▶ **Do you have an English-language menu?**
Eigo-no menyū-wa arimasen-ka.
(Aa-go no men-yuu wah ah-ree-mah-sen kah)
えいごの　メニューはありませんか。

▶ **I'll take Set Meal B, please.**
B-teishoku, onegai-shimasu.
("B" tay-show-kuu oh-nay-guy-she-mahss)
ビーていしょく、おねがいします。

▶ **Tea with milk, please.**
Miruku-tī, kudasai. ミルクティー、ください。
(Me-rue-kuu tee, kuu-dah-sie)

▶ **What kind of fish do you have?**
Donna-sakana-ga arimasu-ka.
(Doan-nah sah-kah-nah gah ah-ree-mahss kah)
どんなさかなが　ありますか。

▶ **Please give me / bring me [something].**
[Something], kudasai. ……、ください。
([something] kuu-dah-sie)

▶ **Thank you for the delicious meal.**
Gochisō-sama-deshita. ごちそうさまでした。
(Go-chee-soe sah-mah desh-tah)

This is a set, institutionalized phrase used to express appreciation when someone treats you to a home meal or pays for your meal or drinks in a restaurant or bar. It is also customary to repeat the expression if you meet the same person a few days later—this time prefacing the phrase with *senjitsu-wa (sen jeet-sue wah)* せんじつは, meaning "the other day."

In Japanese-style restaurants green tea is served without charge. In Chinese restaurants tea is also generally served as part of the meal. In Western-style restaurants normally only black or brown tea is served (straight, with lemon, or with milk), and there is a charge. In addition to the commonly served green tea, there is a higher grade of green tea called *sencha (sen-chah)* せんちゃ, also:

roasted barley tea	*mugi-cha* むぎちゃ *(muu-ghee chah)*
roasted brown tea	*hōji-cha* ほうじちゃ *(hoe-jee chah)*

seaweed (tangle) tea	*kobu-cha* こぶちゃ
	(koe-buu chah)
oolong Chinese tea	*ūron-cha* ウーロンちゃ
	(uu-roan chah)
popped-rice tea	*genmai-cha* げんまいちゃ
	(game-my chah)

▶ **Would you like tea?**
O-cha-wa ikaga-desu-ka. おちゃは　いかがですか。
(Oh-chah wah ee-kah-gah dess kah)

▶ **Yes, please.**
Hai, itadakimasu. はい、いただきます。
(Hie, ee-tah-dah-kee-mahss)

▶ **No thank you.**
Ie, kekkō-desu. いえ、けっこです。
(Ee-eh, keck-koe dess)

Itadakimasu (ee-tah-dah-kee-mahss) いただきます is another set, institutionalized phrase used when accepting food, drink, etc. Japanese mention this just before they start a meal even when it is not someone's treat; in a sense it is the Japanese way of saying grace.

PAYING BILLS

bill	*o-kanjō (oh-kahn-joe)* おかんじょう
receipt	*ryōshūsho* りょうしゅうしょ
	(re-yoe-shuu-show) or
	reshīto (ray-shee-toe) レシート

cash	*genkin (gen-keen)* げんきん
credit card	*kurejitto-kādo* クレジット・カード
	(kuu-ray-jeet-toe kah-doe)

▶ **The bill, please.**
O-kanjō, onegai-shimasu. おかんじょう、おねがいします。
(Oh-kahn-joe oh-nay-guy-she-mahss)

▶ **How much is it altogether?**
Zenbu-de ikura-desu-ka. ぜんぶで　いくらですか。
(Zen-boo day ee-kuu-rah dess kah)

▶ **Can I use a credit card? / Do you take a credit card?**
Kurejitto-kādo-ga tsukaemasu-ka.
(Kuu-ray-jeet-toe kah-doe gah tue-kah-ee-mahss kah)
クレジット・カードが　つかえますか。

▶ **A receipt, please.**
Ryōshūsho, onegai-shimasu.
(Re-yoe-shuu-show oh-nay-guy-she-mahss)
りょうしゅうしょ、おねがいします。

LOCATING RESTROOMS

For the short-term visitor in Japan, locating toilet facilities while out on the town is often a pressing need. Toilets available for public use can be found in major office buildings, usually in the first basement and from the second floor on up; in department stores; and in hotels—also usually in the first basement or the first floor, and on the second-floor and/or mezzanine if there are meeting/banquet rooms on those floors. As in English, there are several Japanese words used to mean toilet.

washroom	*o-tearai* おてあらい
	(oh-tay-ah-rye)—polite term, most common.
toilet	*toire (toe-ee-ray)* トイレ—also widely used, or
	benjo (ben-joe) べんじょ—mainly used by men.
powder room	*keshō-shitsu* けしょうしつ
	(kay-show she-t'sue)
gents	*dansei-yō (dahn-say yoeh)* だんせいよう
ladies	*josei-yō (joe-say yoeh)* じょせいよう

► **Where is the nearest toilet?**
   Ichiban chikai toire-wa doko-desu-ka.
   (Ee-chee-bahn chee-kie toe-ee-ray wah doe-koe dess kah)
   いちばん　ちかい　トイレは　どこですか。

► **Is there a toilet near here?**
   Kono chikaku-ni toire-wa arimasen-ka.
   (Koe-no chee-kah-kuu nee toe-ee-ray wah ah-ree-mah-sen kah)
   この　ちかくに　トイレは　ありませんか。

► **Is there a toilet on this floor?**
   Kono kai-ni toire-wa arimasen-ka.
   (Koe-no kie nee toe-ee-ray wah ah-ree-mah-sen kah)
   この　かいに　トイレは　ありませんか。

► **May I use the toilet?**
   Toire-o karite-mo ii-desu-ka.
   (Toe-ee-ray oh kah-ree-tay moe ee dess kah)
   トイレを　かりても　いいですか。

WHEN SHOPPING

shopping mall	*meiten-gai* めいてんがい *(may-tane guy)*
shopping arcade	*ākēdo* アーケード *(ah-ah-kay-ee-doe)*
shopping street	*shōten-gai* しょうてんがい *(show-tane guy)*
underground mall	*chika-gai (chee-kah guy)* ちかがい
buy	*kaimasu (kie-mahss)* かいます
want to buy	*kaitai-desu* かいたいです *(kie-tie dess)*
look for	*sagashimasu* さがします *(sah-gah-she mass)*
have	*arimasu (ah-ree-mahss)* あります
how much	*ikura (ee-kuu-rah)* いくら
expensive	*takai (tah-kie)* たかい
cheap	*yasui (yah-sue-ee)* やすい
large/big	*ōkii (oh-key)* おおきい
small/little	*chiisai (chee-sie)* ちいさい
more	*motto (moat-toe)* もっと
souvenir	*o-miyage* おみやげ *(oh-me-yah-gay)*
thank you gift	*o-rei (oh-ray)* おれい
mid-year gift	*o-chūgen* おちゅうげん *(oh-chuu-gen)*
end-of-year gift	*o-seibo (oh-say-ee-boe)* おせいぼ
jewelry	*hōseki (hoe-say-kee)* ほうせき
leather	*kawa (kah-wah)* かわ or *rezā (ray-zah)* レザー
book	*hon (koan)* ほん

bookshop　　　　*hon-ya (hoan yah)* ほんや

discount　　　　*waribiki (wah-ree-bee-kee)* わりびき
exchange　　　　*torikae (toe-ree-kah-eh)* とりかえ
written　　　　*setsumei-sho* せつめいしょ
　instructions　　　*(sate-sue-may-ee show)*

▶ **Let's go shopping tomorrow.**
   Ashita kaimono-ni ikimashō.
   (Ah-ssh-tah kie-moe-no nee ee-kee-mah-show)
   あした　かいものに　いきましょう。

▶ **I want to go shopping this afternoon.**
   Kyō-no gogo kaimono-ni ikitai-desu.
   (K'yoe no go-go kie-moe-no nee ee-kee-tie dess)
   きょうの　ごご　かいものに　いきたいです。

▶ **Is there a bookshop around here?**
   Kono hen-ni hon-ya-wa arimasen-ka.
   (Koe-no hen nee hoan-yah wah ah-ree-mah-sen kah)
   この　へんに　ほんやは　ありませんか。

▶ **I am looking for a leather purse.**
   Kawa-no saifu-o sagashite iru-n-desu-kedo.
   *(Kah-wah no sie-who oh sah-gah-ssh-tay ee-ruen dess
   kay-doe)*
   かわの　さいふを　さがして　いるんですけど。

▶ **Do you have jewelry boxes?**
   Hōseki-bako-wa arimasen-ka.
   (Hoe-say-kee bah-koe wah ah-ree-mah-sen kah)
   ほうせきばこは　ありませんか。

▶ **I would like to buy a souvenir.**
O-miyage-o kaitai-n-desu-kedo.
(Oh-me-yah-gay oh kie-tien dess kay-doe)
おみやげを　かいたいんですけど。

▶ **What do you think is good? / What would you recommend?**
Nani-ga ii-to omoimasu-ka.
(Nah-nee gah ee-toe oh-moy-ee-mahss kah)
なにが　いいと　おもいますか。

▶ **Let me see that, please.**
Sore-o misete kudasai. それを　みせて　ください。
(Soe-ray oh me-say-tay kuu-dah-sie)

▶ **Are there other colors?**
Hoka-no iro-ga arimasu-ka.
(Hoe-kah-no ee-roe gah ah-ree-mahss kah)
ほかの　いろが　ありますか。

▶ **May I try it on?**
Kite-mite-mo ii-desu-ka.
(Kee-tay me-tay moh ee-dess kah)
きてみても　いいですか。—used when putting on a shirt, sweater, jacket, and so on.
Haite-mite-mo ii-desu-ka.
(Hie-tay-me-tay-moe ee dess kah)
はいてみても　いいですか。—used when putting on a skirt, trousers, shoes, and so on.

▶ **This is too big. Do you have a smaller one?**
   Kore-wa ōki-sugimasu. Motto chiisai-no-wa arimasen-ka.
   (Koe-ray wah oh-kee-sue-ghee-mahss. Moat-toe chee-sie no wah ah-ree-mah-sen kah)
   これは　おおきすぎます。　もっと　ちいさいのは　あり
   ませんか。

▶ **This one is too expensive. Do you have a cheaper one?**
   Kore-wa taka-sugimasu. Motto yasui-no-wa arimasen-ka.
   (Koe-ray wah tah-kah-sue-ghee-mahss. Moat-toe yah-sue-ee no wah ah-ree-mah-sen kah)
   これは　たかすぎます。　もっと　やすいのは　ありませんか。

▶ **How much is this green box?**
   Kono gurīn-no hako-wa ikura-desu-ka.
   (Koe-no guu-reen no hah-koe wah ee-kuu-rah dess kah)
   この　グリーンの　はこは　いくらですか。

▶ **How much is that one over there?**
   Asoko-ni aru-no-wa ikura-desu-ka.
   (Ah-so-koe nee ah-rue no wah ee-kuu-rah dess kah)
   あそこに　あるのは　いくらですか。

▶ **Which do you think is better?**
   Dochira-ga ii-to omoimasu-ka.
   (Doe-chee-rah gah ee-toe oh-moy-ee-mahss kah)
   どちらが　いいと　おもいますか。

▶ **Are written instructions included?**
   Setsumei-sho-wa tsuite imasu-ka.
   (Sate-sue-may show wah t'sue-ee-tay ee-mahss kah)
   せつめいしょは　ついて　いますか。

▶ **I'll take this, please.**
Kore, kudasai. *(Koe-ray kuu-dah-sie)* これ、ください。

▶ **Can you give me a discount?**
Waribiki-wa dekimasen-ka. わりびきは　できませんか。
(Wah-ree-bee-kee wah day-kee-mah-sen kah)

▶ **Do you allow any discount for cash?**
Genkin-waribiki-wa arimasen-ka.
(Gayn-keen wah-ree-bee-kee wah ah-ree-mah-sen kah)
げんきんわりびきは　ありませんか。

▶ **Is it exchangeable for something else?**
Hoka-no-to torikae-te moraemasu-ka.
(Hoe-kah no toe toe-ree-kah-eh tay moe-rah-eh-mahss kah)
ほかのと　とりかえて　もらえますか。

AT THE STATION

Tickets for both subways and commuter trains are dispensed by vending machines, with the fare on the button to be pushed. There are usually large "fare maps" on the wall above the vending machines, giving the fares to each destination on that particular line as well as on connecting lines.

Unfortunately, most of the destinations are in Japanese characters **kanji** *(kahn-jee)* かんじ. If you cannot read or spot your destination, just buy the cheapest ticket on the machine.

When you get to your destination, go to the Fare-Adjustment Window adjoining the exit turnstiles and hand the ticket to the attendant. He or she will tell you how much extra you must pay, and issue you a new ticket.

Where is the nearest train station?
Ichiban chikai densha-no eki-wa doko-desu-ka?

Board!
Norimasu!

north exit
kita-guchi

Excuse me, does this train stop at Ueno?
Sumimasen. Kono densha-wa Ueno-ni tomarimasu-ka?

 unreserved seat
jiyū-seki

reserved seat ticket
shitei-seki-ken

GREEN CAR
Green Car *gurīn-sha*

Tickets on long-distance trains are generally sold at ticket windows. On "bullet trains," first-class tickets, for coaches that are called "Green Cars," are sold at (you guessed it) "Green Windows" (*midori-no madoguchi* me-doe-ree no mah-doe-guu-chee) みどりの　まどぐち. Green Cars are *gurīn-sha* (guu-reen shah) グリーンしゃ.

station	*eki* (eh-kee) えき
next station	*tsugi-no eki* つぎのえき (t'sue-ghee no eh-kee)
entrance	*iriguchi* (ee-ree-guu-chee) いりぐち
exit	*deguchi* (day guu-chee) でぐち
central exit	*chūō-guchi* ちゅうおうぐち (chuu-oh guu-chee)
west exit	*nishi-guchi* にしぐち (nee-she guu-chee)
east exit	*higashi-guchi* ひがしぐち (he-gah-she guu-chee)
north exit	*kita-guchi* きたぐち (kee-tah guu-chee)
south exit	*minami-guchi* みなみぐち (me-nah-me guu-chee)
escalator	*esukarētā* (ehs-kah-ray-tah) エスカレーター
ticket gate	*kaisatsu-guchi* かいさつぐち (kie-sot-sue guu-chee) or *kaisatsu* (kie-sot-sue) かいさつ
boarding area	*noriba* (no-ree-bah) のりば
boarding platform	*hōmu* (hoe-muu) ホーム

train	*densha (den-shah)* でんしゃ
steam train	*kisha (kee-shah)* きしゃ
long-distance train	*ressha (resh-shah)* れっしゃ
bullet train	*shinkansen* しんかんせん *(sheen-kahn-sen)*
subway	*chikatetsu* ちかてつ *(chee-kah-tet-sue)*
seat	*zaseki (zah-say-kee)* ざせき
unreserved seat	*jiyū-seki* じゆうせき *(jee-yuu say kee)*
reserved seat	*shitei-seki* していせき *(she-tay say-kee)*
smoking seat	*kitsuen-seki* きつえんせき *(kee-t'sue-en say-kee)*
non-smoking seat	*kin'-en-seki* きんえんせき *(keen-en say-kee)*
ticket	*kippu (keep-puu)* きっぷ
ticket sales place	*kippu-uriba* きっぷうりば *(keep-puu uu-ree-bah)*
one-way ticket	*kata-michi-kippu* かたみちきっぷ *(kah-tah me-chee keep-puu)*
round-trip ticket	*ōfuku-kippu* おおふくきっぷ *(ohh-who-kuu keep-puu)*
express ticket	*tokkyū-ken* とっきゅうけん *(toek-queue-ken)*
reserved seat ticket	*shitei-seki-ken* していせきけん *(she-tay say-kee ken)*
departure time	*shuppatsu-jikoku* しゅっぱつじこく *(shupe-pot-sue jee-koe-kuu)*

arrival time	*tōchaku-jikoku* とうちゃくじこく
	(toh-chah-kuu jee-koe-kuu)
transfer	*norikaemasu* のりかえます
	(no-ree-kah-eh-mahss)
board (get on)	*norimasu* *(no-ree-mahss)* のります
disembark (get off)	*orimasu* *(oh-ree-mahss)* おります
stop	*tomarimasu* とまります
	(toe-mah-ree-mahss)

► **Where is the nearest train station?**
   Ichiban chikai densha-no eki-wa doko-desu-ka.
   (Ee-chee-bahn chee-kie den-shah no eh-kee wah doe-koe dess kah)
   いちばん　ちかい　でんしゃの　えきは　どこですか。

► **How much is it to Yokohama?**
   Yokohama-made ikura-desu-ka.
   (Yoe-koe-hah-mah mah-day ee-kuu-rah dess kah)
   よこはままで　いくらですか。

► **What is the platform number for Shinjuku?**
   Shinjuku-yuki-no hōmu-wa nan-ban-desu-ka.
   (Sheen-juu-kuu yuu-kee no hoe-muu wah nahn bahn dess kah)
   しんじゅくゆきの　ホームは　なんばんですか。

► **I want to go to Shibuya. What is the track number?**
   Shibuya-ni ikitai-n-desu-kedo, nan-ban-sen-desu-ka.
   (She-buu-yah nee ee-kee-tien dess kay-doe nahn-bahn-sen dess kah)
   しぶやに　いきたいんですけど、なんばんせんですか。

▶ **Where do I transfer to go to Roppongi?**
Roppongi-ni iku-ni-wa doko-de norikaeta-ra ii-desu-ka.
(Rope-pong-ghee nee ee-kuu nee wah doe-koe day no-ree-kah-eh- tah-rah ee-dess kah)
ろっぽんぎに　いくには　どこで　のりかえたら　いいで
すか。

▶ **Excuse me. Does this train stop at Ueno?**
Suimasen. Kono densha-wa Ueno-ni tomarimasu-ka.
(Suu-ee-mah-sen. Koe-no den-shah wah uu-eh-no nee toe-mah-ree mahss kah)
すいません。この　でんしゃは　うえのに　とまりますか。

▶ **Which exit is the closest to the Keio Plaza Hotel?**
Keiō-Puraza-Hoteru-ni-wa dono deguchi-ga ichiban chikai-desu-ka.
(Kay-oh puu-rah-zah hoe-tay-rue nee wah doe-no day-guu-chee gah ee-chee-bahn chee-kie dess kah)
けいおうプラザホテルには　どの　でぐちが　いちばん
ちかいですか。

VISITING AN OFFICE

company	*kaisha (kie-shah)* かいしゃ	
your company	*onsha (on-shah)* おんしゃ or	
	kisha (kee-shah) きしゃ	
our company	*tōsha (toe-shah)* とうしゃ or	
	heisha (hay-shah) へいしゃ	
office	*jimusho (jee-muu-show)* じむしょ	
	or *ofisu (oh-fee-sue)* オフィス	
address	*jūsho (juu-show)* じゅうしょ	

telephone	*denwa (den-wah)* でんわ
fax	*fakkusu (fak-kuu-sue)* ファックス
	or *fakusu (fa-kuu-sue)* ファクス
number	*bangō (bahn-go)* ばんごう
president	*shachō (shah-choe)* しゃちょう
department head	*buchō (buu-choe)* ぶちょう
section head	*kachō (kah-choe)* かちょう
supervisor	*kakarichō* かかりちょう
	(kah-kah-ree-choe)
floor	*kai (kie)* かい
meeting	*mītingu (me-teen-guu)* ミーティング
	—with one or two people or with a
	visitor/visitors, or *kaigi* かいぎ
	(kie-ghee)—a formal meeting with a
	number of people
appointment	*yakusoku (yahk-soe-kuu)* やくそく
write	*kakimasu (kah-kee-mahss)* かきます

► **What is the name of your company?**
  Onsha-mei-wa nan-deshō-ka.
  (On-shah may wah nahn day-show kah)
  おんしゃめいは　なんでしょうか。

Note that deshō-ka *(day-show kah)* でしょうか is preferred to
desu-ka *(dess kah)* ですか when extra politeness is required.

► **Where is your office?**
  Ofisu-wa dochira-desu-ka. オフィスは　どちらですか。
  (Oh-fee-sue wah doe-chee-rah dess kah)

▶ **What is your address?**
Jūsho-wa dochira-desu-ka.
(Juu-show wah doe-chee-rah dess kah)
じゅうしょは　どちらですか。

▶ **What is your telephone number?**
Denwa-bangō-wa nan-ban-desu-ka.
(Den-wah bahn-go wah nahn-bahn dess kah)
でんわばんごうは　なんばんですか。

▶ **Would you please write it down?**
Kaite itadakemasen-ka. かいて　いただけませんか。
(Kie-tay ee-tah-dah-kay mah-sen kah)

▶ **I will telephone you.**
Denwa-shimasu. (Den-wah she-mahss) でんわします。

▶ **Would you please telephone me?**
Denwa-shite itadakemasen-ka.
(Den-wah she-tay ee-tah-dah-kay mah-sen kah)
でんわして　いただけませんか。

▶ **What floor is your office (on)?**
Ofisu-wa nan-kai-desu-ka.
(Oh-fee-sue wah nahn kie dess kah)
オフィスは　なんかいですか。

▶ **I would like to meet Mr. Saito.**
Saitō-san-ni o-me-ni kakaritai-no-desu-ga.
(Sie-toe-sahn nee oh-may-nee kah-kah-ree-tie no dess gah)
さいとうさんに　おめに　かかりたいのですが。

Note that **tai-no-desu-ga** (tie no dess gah) たいのですが is preferred to **tai-n-desu-kedo** (tien dess kay-doe) たいんですけど when formality is required.

▶ **When will it be convenient for Mr. Saito?**
Saitō-san-wa itsu go-tsugō-ga yoroshii-deshō-ka.
(Sie-toe-sahn wa ee-t'su go-t'sue-go gah yoe-roe-she day-show kah)
さいとうさんは　いつ　ごつごうが　よろしいでしょうか。

▶ **Will 2 p.m. tomorrow be all right?**
Ashita-no gogo ni-ji-de yoroshii-deshō-ka.
(Ah-shh-tah no go-go nee-jee day yoe-roe-she day-show kah)
あしたの　ごご　にじで　よろしいでしょうか。

▶ **That'll be fine.**
Sore-de kekkō-desu. それで　けっこうです。
(So-rei-day keck-koe dess)

▶ **I have an appointment with Mr. Murata at 10 o'clock.**
Jū-ji-ni Murata-san-to yakusoku-ga arimasu.
(Juu-jee nee Muu-rah-tah-sahn toe yahk-soe-kuu gah ah-ree-mahss)
じゅうじに　むらたさんと　やくそくが　あります。

▶ **Where will the meeting with Mr. Murata be held?**
Murata-san-to-no mītingu-wa doko-de arimasu-ka.
(Muu-rah-tah-sahn toe-no me-teen-guu wah doe-koe day ah-ree-mahss kah)
むらたさんとの　ミーティングは　どこで　ありますか。

► **May I use your phone?**
Denwa-o o-kari-shite-mo yoroshii-deshō-ka.
(Den-wah oh oh-kah-ree-she-tay moe yoe-roe-she day-show kah)
でんわを　おかりしても　よろしいでしょうか。

► **May I wait here?**
Koko-de matasete itadaite-mo yoroshii-deshō-ka.
(Koe-koe day mah-tah-say-tay ee-tah-dah-ee-tay mo yoe-roe-she day-show kah)
ここで　またせて　いただいても　よろしいでしょうか。

GETTING CONNECTED

post office	*yūbin-kyoku* ゆうびんきょく *(yuu-bean k'yoe-kuu)*
stamp	*kitte (keet-tay)* きって
envelope	*fūtō (who-toe)* ふうとう
letter	*tegami (tay-gah-me)* てがみ
post card	*hagaki (hah-gah-kee)* はがき
air letter form	*kōkū-shokan* こうくうしょかん *(koe-kuu-show-kahn)*
parcel	*kozutsumi* こづつみ *(koe-zuut-sue-me)*
airmail	*kōkū-bin* こうくうびん *(koe-kuu-bean)*
seamail	*funa-bin (who-nah-bean)* ふなびん
registered mail	*kakitome (kah-kee-toe-may)* かきとめ
special delivery	*sokutatsu (soe-kuu taht-sue)* そくたつ
weight	*omosa (oh-moo-sah)* おもさ or *jūryō (juu-re-yoe)* じゅうりょう

post box	*posuto (poes-toe)* ポスト
mail/post	*dashimasu (dah-she-mahss)* だします
send	*okurimasu* おくります *(oh-kuu-ree-mahss)*

► **Where is the nearest post office?**
Ichiban chikai yūbin-kyoku-wa doko-desu-ka.
(Ee-chee-bahn chee-kie yuu-bean k'yoe-kuu wah doe-koe dess kah)
いちばん　ちかい　ゆうびんきょくは　どこですか。

► **What time does the post office open?**
Yūbin-kyoku-wa nan-ji-ni akimasu-ka.
(Yuu-bean k'yoe-kuu wah nahn-jee nee ah-kee-mahss kah)
ゆうびんきょくは　なんじに　あきますか。

► **What time does it close?**
Nan-ji-ni shimarimasu-ka.
(Nahn-jee nee she-ma-ree-mahss kah)
なんじに　しまりますか。

► **Could I have five 100-yen stamps, please?**
Hyaku-en kitte-o go-mai kudasai.
(H'yah-kuu ehn keet-tay oh go-my kuu-dah-sie)
ひゃくえん　きってを　ごまい　ください。

► **Ten air letter forms, please.**
Kōkū-shokan-o jū-mai kudasai.
(Koe-kuu-show-kahn oh juu-my kuu-dah-sie)
こうくうしょかんを　じゅうまい　ください。

▶ **I would like to send this to the U.S. by special delivery.**
Kore-o Amerika-made sokutatsu-de okuritai-n-desu-kedo.
(Koe-ray oh ah-may-ree-kah mah-day soe-kuu-tot-sue
day oh-kuu-ree-tien dess kay-doe)
これを アメリカまで そくたつで おくりたいんですけど。

▶ **How much will it cost to send this by seamail?**
Kore-wa funa-bin-da-to ikura-ni narimasu-ka.
(Koe-ray wah who-nah-bean dah-toe ee-kuu-rah nee nah-
ree-mahss kah)
これは　ふなびん　だと　いくらに　なりますか。

▶ **How many days will it take for this to get to London?**
Kore-wa London-made nan-nichi-gurai kakarimasu-ka.
(Koe-ray wah roan-doan mah-day nahn nee-chee guu-rye
kah-kah-ree-mahss kah)
これは　ロンドンまで　なんにちぐらい　かかりますか。

▶ **This is printed matter.**
Kore-wa insatsu-butsu-desu.
(Koe-ray wah een-sah-t'sue-boo-t'sue dess)
これは　いんさつぶつです。

THE INTERNET

computer	*konpyūtā* コンピューター
	(kon-pew-tar) or
	pasokon (pah-so-kon) パソコン
laptop	*nōto-pasokon* ノートパソコン
	(noh-toe-pah-so-kon)
Wifi	*wai-fai (wi fi)* ワイ・ファイ

password	*pasuwādo (pass-wahd)* パスワード
email	*denshi-mēru* でんしメール
	(den-she may-rue) or
	ī-mēru (ee may-rue) イーメール
email address	*mēru-adoresu* メールアドレス
	(may-rue ado-ress)
Internet	*Intānetto (intah-netoh)* インターネット
download	*daunrōdo (down-roado)* ダウンロード
website	*websaito (web-sigh-to)* ウェブサイト
error message	*erā-messēji* エラーメッセージ
	(eraa mays-say-jee)
virus	*uirusu (wai-ras)* ウイルス
turn on	*konpyūtā-no dengen-o ireru*
(computer)	*(kon-pew-tar no dengen oh ear-re-rue)*
	コンピューターの　でんげんを　いれる
shut down	*konpyūtā-no dengen-o kiru*
(computer)	*(kon-pew-tar no dengen oh kee-rue)*
	コンピューターの　でんげんを　きる
log on	*rog-on suru* ログオンする
	(rog on sue-rue)
log off	*rog-ofu suru* ログオフする
	(rog off sue-rue)
scroll up/down	*sukurōru-appu/daun suru*
	(sue-kue-row-rue appu/down sue-rue)
	スクロールアップ/ダウンする
screen	*gamen (ga-men)* がめん
display monitor	*monitā (moe-nee-tar)* モニター
mouse	*maus (mou-sue)* マウス
click the mouse	*maus-o kurikku suru*
	(mou-sue oh ku-rikku sue-rue)
	マウスをクリックする

▶ **Do you have Wi-fi?**
Wai-fai-ga arimasu-ka.
(Wi-fi gah ah-ree-mahss kah)
ワイ・ファイが　ありますか。

▶ **Could you tell me the Wi-fi password?**
Wai-fai pasuwādo-o oshiete kudasai.
(Wi-fi pass-wahd oh osh-ee-ay-tay kuu-dah-sie)
ワイ・ファイ パスワードを　おしえてください。

▶ **Could I have your email address?**
Mēru-adoresu-o oshiete kudasai.
(May-rue ado-ress oh osh-ee-ay-tay kuu-dah-sie)
メールアドレスを　おしえてください。

▶ **Did you get my email?**
Watashi-no mēru todokimashita-ka.
(Wah-tah-she no may-rue toh-doh-ki-mahsshtah)
わたしの　メール　とどきましたか。

▶ **There's something wrong with this computer.**
Kono-konpyūtā-wa doko-ka okashii-desu.
(Koe-no kon-pew-tar wah doe-koe gah oe-kah-she dess)
この　コンピューターは　どこか　おかしいです。

▶ **I can't connect to the Internet.**
Intānetto-ni setsuzoku dekimasen.
(Intah-netoh nee setsu-zokue day-kee-mah-sen)
インターネットに　せつぞく　できません。

► **I can't download this page.**
Kono pēji-o daunrōdo dekimasen.
(Koe-noe pay-jee oh down-roado day-kee-mah-sen)
この　ページを　ダウンロード　できません。

► **What's the website address?**
Websaito-no adoresu-wa nan-desu-ka.
(Web-sigh-to no ado-ress wah nan dess-kah)
ウェブサイトの　アドレスは　なんですか。

► **I'm getting an error message.**
Erā-messēji-ga demashita.
(Eraa mays-say-jee gah day-mahsshtah)
エラーメッセージが　でました。

► **My computer froze.**
Pasokon-ga furīzu-shimashita.
(Pah-so-kon gah fuh-ree-zu she-mahsshtah)
パソコンが　フリーズしまた。

MEDICAL EMERGENCIES

sickness	*byōki (be-yoe-kee)* びょうき
	—serious enough to see a doctor.
symptom	*shōjō (show-joe)* しょうじょう
feel bad	*guai-ga warui* ぐあいが　わるい
	(g'wie gah wah-rue-ee)
have a headache	*atama-ga itai* あたまが　いたい
	(ah-tah-mah gah ee-tie)
have a toothache	*ha-ga itai* はが　いたい
	(hah gah ee-tie)

have a stomachache	*onaka-ga itai* おなかが　いたい *(oh-nah-kah gah ee-tie)*
have diarrhea	*geri-o shite imasu* *(gay-ree oh ssh-tay ee-mahss)* げりを　して　います
have a fever	*netsu-ga arimasu* *(nay-t'sue gah ah-ree-mahss)* ねつが　あります
feel nausea	*hakike-ga shimasu* *(hah-kee-kay gah she-mahss)* はきけが　します
catch a cold	*kaze-o hikimasu* *(kah-zay oh he-kee-mahss)* かぜを　ひきます
get injured	*kega-o shimasu* けがを　します *(kay-gah oh she-mahss)*
doctor	*isha (ee-shah)* いしゃ
dentist	*haisha (hah-ee-shah)* はいしゃ
hospital	*byōin (b'yoeh-een)* びょういん
clinic	*kurinikku* クリニック *(kuu-ree-neek-kuu)* or *shinryōjo* しんりょうじょ *(sheen-re-yoe-joe)*
examination	*shinsatsu (sheen-sot-sue)* しんさつ
operation	*shujutsu* しゅじゅつ *(shuu-juute-sue)*
blood pressure	*ketsuatsu* けつあつ *(kay-t'sue ah-t'sue)*
bandage	*hōtai (hoe-tie)* ほうたい
insurance	*hoken (hoe-ken)* ほけん
health insurance	*kenkō-hoken (ken-koe hoe-ken)* けんこうほけん

medicine	*kusuri (kuu-sue-ree)* くすり
drugstore	*kusuri-ya* くすりや
	(kuu-sue-ree-yah) or
	yakkyoku (yahk-q'yoe-koo) やっきょく
ambulance	*kyūkyūsha (queue-queue-shah)*
	きゅうきゅうしゃ

become	*nyūin-shimasu* にゅういんします
hospitalised	*(knew-een she-mahss)*
leave the	*taiin-shimasu* たいいんします
hospital	*(tah-ee-een-she-mahss)*

▶ **I am sick. Please call a doctor.**
Guai-ga warui-desu. Isha-o yonde kudasai.
(G'wie gah wah-rue-ee dess. Ee-shah oh yoan-day kuu-dah-sie)
ぐあいが　わるいです。　いしゃを　よんで　ください。

▶ **Please call an ambulance.**
Kyūkyūsha-o yonde kudasai.
(Queue-queue-shah oh yoan-day kuu-dah-sie)
きゅうきゅうしゃを　よんでください。

▶ **(Someone) has been hurt in an accident.**
Jiko-de kega-o shimashita.
(Jee-koe day kay-gah oh she-mah-ssh-tah)
じこで　けがを　しました。

▶ **Please help (me, us)!**
Tasukete kudasai. たすけて　ください。
(Tahss-kate-tay kuu-dah-sie)

▶ **I caught a cold.**
Kaze-o hikimashita. かぜを　ひきました。
(Kah-zay oh he-kee-mah-ssh-tah)

▶ **What symptoms do you have?**
Donna shōjō-ga arimasu-ka.
(Doen-na show-joe gah ah-ree-mass kah)
どんな　しょうじょうが　ありますか。

▶ **I have a stomachache. And I am suffering from diarrhea.**
Onaka-ga itai-desu. Sorekara, geri-o shite imasu.
(Oh-nah-kah gah ee-tie dess. So-ray-kah-rah, gay-ree oh ssh-tay ee-mahss)
おなかが　いたいです。　それから、げりを　しています。

▶ **I have a terrible headache. Do you have any aspirin?**
Atama-ga hidoku itai-desu. Asupirin-wa arimasen-ka.
(Ah-tah-mah gah he-doe-kuu ee-tie dess. Ah-sue-pee-reen wah ah-ree-mah-sen kah)
あたまが　ひどく　いたいです。アスピリンは　ありませんか。

IN THE BATH

In Japan people share the same water when they take a bath at home and in Japanese-style hotels (*ryokan (re-yoe kahn)*りょかん). It is absolutely necessary to wash your body before you get in the tub so that the water stays clean until the last person takes a bath.

bath   *furo (who-roe)* ふろ or more politely,
        o-furo (oh-who-roe) おふろ

bathroom	*yokushitu (yoe-kuu-she-t'sue)* よくしつ or *furo-ba (who-roe-bah)* ふろば
bathrobe	*basurōbu (bah-sue-roe-buu)* バスローブ
Japanese bathrobe	*yukata (yuu-kah-tah)* ゆかた
soap	*sekken (sake-ken)* せっけん
shampoo	*shanpū (shahm-poo)* シャンプー
towel	*taoru (tah-aw-rue)* タオル
bath towel	*basutaoru* バスタオル *(bah-sue-tah-aw-rue)*
hot water	*o-yu (oh-yuu)* おゆ
cold water	*mizu (me-zuu)* みず
shower	*shawā (shah-wah)* シャワー
take a bath	*o-furo-ni hairimasu (oh-whoroe nee hie-ree-mahss)* おふろに　はいります
take a shower	*shawā-o abimasu (shah-wah oh ah-bee-mahss)* シャワーを　あびます
public bath	*sentō (sen-toe)* せんとう
hotspring spa	*onsen (own-sen)* おんせん
mixed-sex bathing	*kon'yoku (kone-yoe-kuu)* こんよく
open-air bath	*roten-buro* ろてんぶろ *(roe-ten buu-roe)*

▶ **Shall we take a bath now?**
Sorosoro o-furo-ni hairimashō-ka.
(So-roe so-roe oh-who-roe nee hie-ree-mah-show-kah)
そろそろ　おふろに　はいりましょうか。

▶ **I want to take a shower.**
Shawā-o abitai-desu. シャワーを　あびたいです。
(Shah-wah oh ah-bee-tie dess)

▶ **Do you have any soap?**
Sekken-wa arimasen-ka. せっけんは　ありませんか。
(Sake-ken wah ah-ree-mah-sen kah)

▶ **This (water) is too hot.**
Kore-wa atsu-sugimasu. これは　あつすぎます。
(Koe-ray wah aht-sue sue-ghee-mahss)

▶ **Is it all right to put in a little cold water?**
Sukoshi mizu-o tashite-mo ii-desu-ka.
(Sue-koe-she me-zuu oh tah-she-tay moe ee-dess kah)
すこし　みずを　たしても　いいですか。

▶ **This is not hot enough.**
Kore-wa nurui-desu. これは　ぬるいです。
(Koe-ray wah nuu-rue-ee dess)

▶ **Is it all right to put in a little hot water?**
Sukoshi o-yu-o tashite-mo ii-desu-ka.
(Sue-koe-she oh-yuu oh tah-she-tay moe ee-dess kah)
すこし　おゆを　たしても　いいですか。

HOUSING

apartment　　*apāto (ah-pah-toe)* アパート
condominium　*manshon (mahn-shone)* マンション
　　　　　　　　—from "mansion"

rental home	*kashi-ya (kah-she yah)* かしや
	—from a landlord's point of view, or
	shakuya (shah-kuu-yah) しゃくや
	—from a tenant's point of view.
rent	*yachin (yah-cheen)* やちん
rental agent	*fudōsan-ya* ふどうさんや
	(who-doe-sahn yah)
guarantor	*hoshō-nin* ほしょうにん
	(hoe-show-neen)
deposit	*hoshō-kin* ほしょうきん
(guarantee)	*(hoe-show-keen)*
deposit (earnest)	*shiki-kin (she-kee-keen)* しききん
gift money	*rei-kin (ray-keen)* れいきん
handling	*tesū-ryo* てすうりょう
charge	*(tay sue-re-yoe)*
lease contract	*chintai-keiyaku* ちんたいけいやく
	(cheen-tie-kay-yah-kuu)
signature	*shomei (show-may)* しょめい or
	sain (sine) サイン
floor mats	*tatami (tah-tah-me)* たたみ
one tatami	*ichi-jō (ee-chee-joe)* いちじょう
area	—approximately 18 square feet
room/land	*tsubo (t'sue-boe)* つぼ
area unit	= 2 *jō (nee-joe)*
view	*miharashi (me-hah-rah-she)* みはらし
residential	*jūtaku-chi* じゅうたくち
area	*(juu-tah-kuu chee)*
with bath	*furo-tsuki* ふろつき
	(who-roe t'sue-kee)
dining & kitchen	*dī-kē (dee-kay / DK)* ディーケー
lounge, dining &	*eru-dī-kē (eh-rue-dee-kay / LDK)*
kitchen	エルディーケー

In Japan room-size is usually measured in **_tatami_** *(tah-tah-me)*
たたみ mats, the traditional Japanese flooring. One mat is
approximately 3-feet by 6-feet, and in this context is called a
_jō_ *(joe)* じょう—a **_roku-jō_** *(roe-kuu-joe)* ろくじょう room is a
six-mat room, or 108 square feet; a **_jū-jō_** *(juu-joe)* じゅうじょう
room is a 10-mat room with 180 square feet of space.

Larger rooms, such as offices, and plots of land are normally measured in **_tsubo_** *(t'sue-boe)* つぼ which equals two
tatami *(tah-tah-me)* たたみ mats or two **_jō_**. A **_30-tsubo_** *(sahn-
juut-t'sue-boe)* さんじゅっつぼ house has 1,080 square feet of
space.

► **I want to rent an apartment.**
  Apāto-o karitai-n-desu-kedo.
  (Ah-pah-toe oh kah-ree-tien dess kay-doe)
  アパートを　かりたいんですけど。

► **How much is the monthly rent?**
  Maitsuki-no yachin-wa ikura-desu-ka.
  (My t'sue-kee no yah-cheen wah ee-kuu-rah dess kah)
  まいつきの　やちんは　いくらですか。

► **How many mats does the room have?**
  Heya-wa nan-jō-desu-ka.
  (Hay-yah wah nahn joe dess kah)
  へやは　なんじょうですか。

► **Does it have a bath?**
  Furo-wa tsuite imasu-ka. ふろは　ついて　いますか。
  (Who-roe wah t'sue-ee-tay ee-mahss kah)

▶ **Does it have a view?**
Miharashi-wa ii-desu-ka. みはらしは　いいですか。
(Me-hah-rah-she wah ee-dess kah)

▶ **How many rooms does it have?**
Nan-dī-kē-desu-ka. なん DK ですか。
(Nahn dee-kay/DK dess kah)

This is a commonly used expression to ask how many rooms the property has in addition to a dining room and a kitchen. *Nan-eru-dī-kē-desu-ka (nahn LDK dess kah)* なんLDKですか is used instead when the property has a lounge as well, and *nan-kē-desu-ka (nahn kay/K dess kah)* なんKですか when there is only a kitchen.

▶ **I am looking for a 2DK apartment.**
Nī-dī-kē-no apāto-o sagashite imasu.
(Nee DK no ah-pah-toe oh sah-gah-she-tay ee-mahss)
2DKの　アパートを　さがしています。

AGE

age	*toshi (toe-she)* とし or
	nenrē (nen-ray) ねんれい
years old	*sai (sie)* さい
child	*kodomo (koe-doe-moe)* こども
adult	*otona (oh-toe-nah)* おとな
elderly person	*o-toshiyori* おとしより
	(oh-toe-she-yoe-ree)
young	*wakai (wah-kie)* わかい

old   *toshi-o-totta* としをとった
                    (toe-she oh toettah)

▶ **How old are you?**
  Nan-sai-desu-ka. なんさいですか。
  (Nahn sie dess kah)
  O-ikutsu-desu-ka. おいくつですか。
  (Oh-ee-kuut-sue dess kah)

Note that asking the listener his/her age is rude in Japan so
you must avoid it unless absolutely necessary.

▶ **I am 40 years old.**
  Watashi-wa yon-jus-sai-desu.
  (Wah-tah-she wah yone-juus sie dess)
  わたしは　よんじゅっさいです。

▶ **My son is 15 years old.**
  Musuko-wa jū-go-sai-desu.
  (Muu-sue-koe wah juu-go sie dess)
  むすこは　じゅうごさいです。

IN A BAR

beer	*bīru (bee-rue)* ビール
black beer	*kuro-bīru (kuu-roe bee-rue)* くろビール
draught/ draft beer	*nama-bīru* なまビール *(nah-mah bee-rue)*
lager beer	*ragā-bīru* ラガービール *(rah-gah bee-rue)*
light beer	*raito-bīru (rye-toe bee-rue)* ライトビール

alcohol-free beer	*non-arukōru-bīru* ノンアルコールビール
	(non-ah-rue-koe-rue bee-rue)
cocktail	*kakuteru (kah-koo-tay-rue)* カクテル
rice wine	*o-sake (oh-sah-kay)* おさけ or
	nihon-shu (nee-hoan-shuu) にほんしゅ
wine	*wain (wah-een)* ワイン
scotch	*sukotchi (sue-koet-chee)* スコッチ
whisky	*uisukī (uu-ees-kee)* ウイスキー
bourbon	*bābon (bah-bone)* バーボン
brandy	*burandē (boo-ran-dey)* ブランデー
gin	*jin (jeen)* ジン
vodka	*wokka (uu-oh-kah)* ウォッカ
highball	*haibōru (high-boe-rue)* ハイボール
[something] with water	[something]-*no mizu-wari*
	[something] *(no mee-zoo wah-ree)*
	……の　みずわり
on-the-rocks	*on-za-rokku (on-zah-roke-kuu)*
	オンザロック
strong (drinker)	*sake-ni tsuyoi* さけに　つよい
	(sah-kay nee t'sue-yoe-ee)
weak (drinker)	*sake-ni yowai* さけに　よわい
	(sah-kay nee yoe-wah-ee)
beer garden	*biya-gāden* ビヤガーデン
	(bee-yah gahh-den)
hangover	*futsuka-yoi* ふつかよい
	(whoots-kah-yoe-e)

▶ **Kirin beer, please.**
   Kirin-bīru, kudasai. キリンビール、ください。
   (Kee-reen bee-rue kuu-dah-sie)

► **Do you have draft beer?**
Nama-bīru-wa arimasu-ka.
(Nah-mah bee-rue wah ah-ree-mahss kah)
なまビールは　ありますか。

► **Another round, please.**
O-kawari, kudasai おかわり、ください。
(Oh-kah-wah-ree kuu-dah-sie)

► **Some tidbits (peanuts, etc.), please.**
O-tsumami, kudasai. おつまみ、ください。
(Oh-t'sue-mah-me kuu-dah-sie)

In some cabarets and clubs, patrons are automatically served a platter of tidbits that may range from tiny sandwiches to mixed peanuts and *arare* (ah-rah-ray) あられ "bean-sized rice crackers." This "service" is called *chāmu* (cha-muu) チャーム from "charm," and is aimed at helping to set a convivial mood. There is a charge for the *chāmu* (cha-muu) チャーム.

TELEPHONES AND TEXTING

telephone	*denwa (dane-wah)* でんわ
cell-phone	*keitai-denwa* けいたいでんわ
	(kay-tie-dane-wah) or
	keitai (kay-tie) けいたい
smartphone	*sumaho (sue-mah-ho)* スマホ
domestic	*kokunai-denwa* こくないでんわ
phone call	*(koe-kuu-nie den-wah)*
long	*chō-kyori-denwa* ちょうきょりでんわ
distance call	*(choe-k'yoe-ree den-wah)*

international call	*kokusai-denwa* こくさいでんわ *(koke-sie den-wah)*
telephone number	*denwa-bangō* でんわばんごう *(den-wah bahn-go)*
extension	*naisen (nie-sen)* ないせん
make call / phone	*denwa-o kakemasu* *(den-wah oh kah-kay-mahss)* でんわを　かけます or *denwa-o shimasu* でんわを　します *(den-wah oh she-mahss)*
busy phone	*hanashi-chū* はなしちゅう *(hah-nahss-chew)*
hello	*moshi-moshi* もしもし *(moe-she-moe-she)*

Moshi-moshi (moe-she-moe-she) もしもし is the "telephone hello," which is an abbreviation for *mōshiagemasu mōshiagemasu* "I am going to tell you, I am going to tell you."

► **You have a phone call.**
   O-denwa-desu. (Oh-den-wah dess) おでんわです

► **Just a moment, please.**
   Shō-shō o-machi-kudasai.
   (Show-show oh-mah-chee kuu-dah-sie)
   しょうしょう　おまちください。

► **Who is calling, please?**
   Dochira-sama-deshō-ka. どちらさまでしょうか。
   (Doe-chee-rah sah-mah day-show kah)

▶ **Is Mr. Tanaka in?**
Tanaka-san-wa irasshaimasu-ka.
(Tah-nah-kah-sahn wah ee-rash-shy-mahss kah)
たなかさんは　いらっしゃいますか。

▶ **He is away from his desk.***
Seki-o hazushite orimasu.
(Say-kee oh hah-zuu-sshtay oh-ree-mahss)
せきを　はずして　おります。

▶ **He/she is out now.***
Tadaima gaishutsu-shite orimasu.
(Tah-die-mah gie-shuu-t'sue she-tay-oh-ree mahss)
ただいま　がいしゅつして　おります。

▶ **He/she is on another line.***
Hoka-no denwa-ni dete orimasu.
(Hoe-kah-no den-wah nee day-tay oh-ree-mahss)
ほかの　でんわに　でて　おります。

▶ **He/she is in a meeting now.***
Tadaima kaigi-chū-desu.
(Tah-dah ee-mah kie-ghee-chuu dess)
ただいま　かいぎちゅうです。

*Ga *(gah)* が is usually added after these expressions when
said on the phone in order to avoid bluntness.

▶ **Shall I get him/her to call you?**
O-denwa-sasemashō-ka. おでんわさせましょうか。
(Oh-den-wah sah-say-mah-show kah)

▶ **Please tell him I called.**
O-denwa-sashiageta-koto-o o-tsutae-kudasai.
(Oh-den-wah sah-she-ah-gay-tah koe-toe oh oh-t'sue-tah-eh kuu-dah-sie)
おでんわ　さしあげたことを　おつたえください。

▶ **Would you like me to call you or text you?**
Denwa-to messēji, dochira-no-hō-ga ii-desu-ka.
(Den-wha toe may-say-jee doe-chee-rah no hoe gah ee dess kah)
でんわと　メッセージ、どちらのほうが　いいですか。

▶ **When I get to Shinjuku station, I will text you.**
Shinjuku-eki-ni tsuitara mēru-shimasu.
(Sheen-jew-koo ee-key nee tsu-ee-taw-rah meh-roo she-mah-sue)
しんじゅくえきに　ついたら　メールします。

▶ **Which smartphone is the cheapest?**
Dono sumaho-ga ichiban yasui-desu-ka.
(Doe-no sue-mah-ho gah ee-chee-bahn yah-sue-ee dess kah)
どの　スマホが　いちばん　やすいですか。

▶ **Do you have the charger for this cell phone?**
Kono keitai-no jūdenki motte-imasu-ka.
(Koh-no kay-tie no jew-den-key mowt-tay-ee-mahss kah)
この　けいたいの　じゅうでんき　もっていますか。

▶ **My phone has no cell service.**
Denpa-ga arimasen. でんぱ-が　ありません。
(Den-paw gah ah-ree-mah-sen)

▶ **We will use the smartphone GPS to go to the hot spring.**
Sumaho-no nabi-o tsukatte, onsen-ni ikimasu.
(Sue-mah-ho no naw-bee oh tsu-kah-tay, own-sen nee ee-key-mahs)
スマホの　ナビを　つかって、おんせんに　いきます。

▶ **I'll check on my phone to see where we can eat.**
Doko-de taberu-ka sumaho-de shirabemasu.
(Doe-koo day tah-beh-rue-kah sue-mah-ho day she-rah-beh-mah-sue)
どこで　たべるか　スマホで　しらべます。

VISITING A HOME

Again there are specific institutionalized phrases that are used when visiting Japanese homes. In their order of use they are as follows:

gomen-kudasai (go-men kuu-dah-sie) ごめんください
This more or less means "please excuse me" and is used to announce one's self at the door or after entering the foyer, if there is no doorbell. You might say it is the Western equivalent of knocking on a door or calling out a very polite "hello." In traditional Japanese homes in earlier years, outer gates and doors were generally unlocked during the day, allowing callers to enter the *genkan (gen-khan)* げんかん or vestibule before announcing themselves. It is used in the same way today both at private homes and at offices where there is no doorbell or receptionist.

o-jama-shimasu *(oh-jah-mah she-mahss)* おじゃまします
After you have been invited into a home, and make the first
move to enter, it is customary to say ***o-jama-shimasu*** *(oh-jah-
mah she-mahss)* おじゃまします, meaning "I am intruding" or
"I am bothering you."

itadakimasu *(ee-tah-dah-kee-mahss)* いただきます
When served any kind of drink or food, it is customary to say,
itadakimasu *(ee-tah-dah-kee-mahss)* いただきます just before
you start drinking or eating. It literally means "receive" and is
used almost like a prayer, in the figurative sense of "I receive/
accept *(this with thanks)*."

gochisō-sama-deshita ごちそうさまでした
(go-chee-soe sah-mah desh-tah)
Gochisō *(go-chee-soe)* ごちそう means "treat" or "entertainment"; ***sama*** *(sah-mah)* さま is an honorific term for "Miss,
Mr. or Mrs." and in this case is used in reference to the host.
The colloquial sense is "thank you very much for the delicious
food/drinks."

o-jama-shimashita おじゃましました
(oh-jah-mah she-mah-sshtah)
The past tense of "I am intruding," this is used when departing
from a home or office. Frequently with ***dōmo*** *(doe-moe)* どう
も, in this case meaning "very," in front of it, as in ***dōmo o-
jama-shimashita*** *(doe-moe oh-jah-mah she-mah-sshtah)* どう
も　おじゃましました。

EXPRESSING THANKS

thanks	***dōmo*** *(doe-moe)* どうも or ***arigatō*** *(ah-ree-gah-toe)* ありがとう
thank you	***arigatō gozaimasu*** *(ah-ree-gah-toe go-zie-mahss)* ありがとう　ございます* or ***arigatō gozaimashita*** *(ah-ree-gah-toe go-zie-mah-sshtah)* ありがとう　ございました*
thank you very much	***dōmo arigatō gozaimasu*** *(doe-moe ah-ree-gah-toe go-zie-mahss)* どうも　ありがとう　ございます* or ***dōmo arigatō gozaimashita*** *(doe-moe ah-ree-gah-toe go-zie-mah-sshtah)* どうも　ありがとう　ございました*

*The non-past tense with **-masu** *(-mahss)* ます is said immediately after a short-term favor, while the past tense with **-mashita** *(-mah-sshtah)* ました is said when a long-term favor is finally over or some time after the short/long-term favor (e.g. a few hours/days later).

excuse me/ thank you	***sumimasen*** すみません *(sue-me-mah-sen)* or ***dōmo sumimasen*** どうもすみません *(doe-moe sue-me-mah-sen)*

The term the Japanese use most often to express gratitude is ***sumimasen*** *(sue-me-mah-sen)* すみません, which primarily expresses the concept of an apology, "I'm sorry." The reason for expressing gratitude by means of apology is the feeling they have when they have received a favor—"I should not have caused you trouble to do this for me. I am sorry, but I do appreciate it."

Sumimasen (sue-me-mah-sen) すみません is also the term most frequently used in restaurants and other places of business to attract the attention of waiters and others.

Sumimasen-ga (sue-me-mah-sen gah) すみませんが customarily prefaces any approach to clerks, policemen, officials, etc., when one has a question or a request.

thanks to you   *o-kage-sama-de* おかげさまで
                    (oh-kah-gay-sah-mah day)

When asked how they are or how they enjoyed a trip or when congratulated on a happy event, Japanese will often preface their thanks with the set phrase *o-kage-sama-de (oh-kah-gay-sah-mah day)* おかげさまで, which means "thanks to you"—e.g. *o-kage-sama-de genki-desu (oh-kah-gay sah-mah day gen-kee dess)* おかげさまで　げんきです or "thanks to you, I'm fine," and *o-kage-sama-de tanoshii-ryokō-deshita (oh-kah-gay sah-mah day tah-no-she rio-koe desh-tah)* おかげさまで　たのしいりょこうでした or "thanks to you, it was an enjoyable trip."

▶ **Thanks to you I had a wonderful evening.**
  O-kage-sama-de konban-wa totemo tanoshikatta-desu.
  (Oh-kah-gay sah-mah day kome-bahn wa toe-tay-moe tah-no-she-kattah dess)
  おかげさまで　こんばんは　とても　たのしかったです。

▶ **I very much appreciate your kindness.**
Go-shinsetsu-o fukaku kansha-shimasu.
(Go-sheen-set-sue oh who-kah-kuu kahn-shah she-mahss)
ごしんせつを　ふかく　かんしゃします。

▶ **Thank you for the meal / drinks.**
*Gochisō-sama-deshita.** ごちそうさまでした。
(Go-chee-so sah-mah desh-tah)

*This institutionalized phrase is said to your host in his/her home, as well as anywhere else after eating or drinking at his or her expense.

▶ **Thank you, I've had enough.**
Mō kekkō-desu. もう　けっこうです。
(Moh keck-koe dess)

▶ **Thank you for your help / assistance.**
O-sewa-ni narimashita. おせわに　なりました。
(Oh-say-wah nee nah-ree-mah-sshtah)
Tasukarimashita. たすかりました。
(Tah-sue-kah-ree mah-sshtah)

▶ **I am very grateful to you (for what you have done for me).**
Taihen arigataku omotte imasu.
(Tie-hen ah-ree-gah-tah-kuu oh-mot-tay ee-mahss)
たいへん　ありがたく　おもっています。

▶ **Don't mention it. / You're welcome.**
Dō itashimashite. どう　いたしまして。
(Doe ee-tah-she-mah-sshtay)

▶ **Not at all.**
Iie. (Ee-eh) いいえ。

APOLOGIZING

Given their highly sophisticated and deeply entrenched system of personal etiquette, which resulted in extreme sensitivity to verbal and behaviorial slights, the Japanese are always apologizing out of cultural force of habit (the key word for expressing thanks—*sumimasen (sue-me-mah-sen)* すみません—is also an apology).

Most formal acts begin with an apology; speeches begin with an apology; even many casual conversations begin with an apology—almost always the dual-purpose *sumimasen (sue-me-mah-sen)* すみません .

▶ **Excuse me / I'm sorry.**
Sumimasen. (Sue-me-mah-sen) すみません。
Gomen-nasai. (Go-mane-nah-sie) ごめんなさい。

Note that the latter is less formal than the former. Children almost exclusively use the latter and women tend to use it far more often than men.

▶ **I am terribly sorry.**
Mōshiwake arimasen. もうしわけ　ありません。
(Moh-she-wah-kay ah-ree-mah-sen)
Shitsuree-shimashita. しつれいしました。
(She-t'sue-ray she-mah-sshtah)

These terms are more formal than *sumimasen (sue-me-mah-sen)* すみません and are opted for in business and in formal situations,

▶ **Please forgive me.**
   Yurushite kudasai. ゆるして　ください。
   (Yuu-rue-ssh-tay kuu-dah-sie)

In usage, *gomen-nasai (go-mane-nah-sie)* ごめんなさい, often expressed in personal situations as *gomen-ne (go-mane nay)* ごめんね, is the weakest of the above terms, and it is most often heard in very casual situations. Mothers say it to their young children. Teenage girls say it to each other. Adults sometimes use it in a teasing manner as well as on more serious occasions. The strength of its meaning is primarily determined by the demeanor and voice of the individual apologizing.
   Gomen-nasai (go-mane-nah-sie) ごめんなさい and *sumimasen (sue-me-mah-sen)* すみません are interchangeable in many situations when used as an apology. However, when saying "excuse me" to attract someone's attention, it is always *sumimasen (sue-me-mah-sen)* すみません, which is often pronounced as *suimasen (sue-ee-mah-sen)* すいません .

SAYING GOODBYE

goodbye	*sayōnara (sah-yoe-nah-rah)* さようなら
	(The literal meaning is "if it must be so.")
take care	*ki-o tsukete* きを　つけて
	(kee oh t'sue-kay-tay)

When parting for an extended period of time, other commonly used terms are:

o-genki-de (*oh-gane-kee day*) おげんきで
go-kigen-yō (*go-kee-gane yoe*) ごきげんよう

Both of these phrases mean something like "be in good health."

When leaving someone who has been sick or whose health is fragile, the following is said:

o-daiji-ni (*oh-die-jee-nee*) おだいじに

It is another expression of "take care."

When people are seeing a business associate off for a distant or overseas assignment—or when sending newlyweds off on their honeymoon—they will ceremoniously shout **BANZAI!** (*bahn-zie*) ばんざい three times, each time throwing their hands up in the air.

This shout has traditionally been used as a greeting to the Emperor (**tennō-heika banzai** *tane-no hay-ee-kah bahn-zie*) てんのうへいか　ばんざい which translates as "Long Live His Imperial Majesty," and as the equivalent of "Charge!" when employed by warriors, soldiers, and other military forces when attacking an enemy. When used today as a farewell, the meaning is something like "Hip! Hip! Hooray!"

PART TWO
Places

KEY NAMES & PLACES

A significant part of the communication barrier visitors experience shortly after arriving in Japan—besides not being able to speak or understand Japanese—is the inability to pronounce common Japanese place-names and words. In some cases, this inability includes not being able to pronounce the names of the hotels where they are staying, which is about as basic as you can get.

Learning how to pronounce words is, of course, a lot easier than learning how to "speak" Japanese, but it is still a key part of becoming "fluent" in daily life in the country.

Try pronouncing the following words with special attention to the length of long vowels and the moraic nasal. When you do, make sure to suppress your typical English stress accent. (Remember that Japanese is a language with a pitch accent?) Even if your use of pitch is not right, people should still be able to understand you, but if you use stress for accentuation, you may have a very hard time making yourself understood. Good luck.

COUNTRY, ISLANDS & REGIONS

Japan / Japanese

Japan	*Nihon* (nee-hone)
Japanese (person)	*Nihon-jin* (nee-hone-jeen)
Japanese (language)	*Nihon-go* (nee-hone-go)

The Islands

Hokkaido	*Hokkaidō* (hoke-kie-doe)
Honshu	*Honshū* (hone-shuu)
Shikoku	*Shikoku* (she-koe-kuu)
Kyushu	*Kyūshū* (queue-shuu)
Okinawa	*Okinawa* (oh-kee-nah-wah)

Regions

Tohoku (six prefectures of northern Honshu)
Tōhoku (toe-hoe-kuu)

Kanto (six prefectures around Tokyo)
Kantō (kahn-toe)

Chubu (nine prefectures in central Honshu)
Chūbu (chuu-buu)

Kinki (seven prefectures around Kyoto-Osaka)
Kinki (keen-kee)

Chugoku (five prefectures in western Honshu)
Chūgoku (chuu-go-kuu)

There are three other geographically and economically defined regions of Japan, made up of the islands of Hokkaido, Shikoku, and Kyushu. A district name that one hears constantly is ***Kansai*** *(kahn-sie)* かんさい, which refers to the Osaka-Kobe area.

PREFECTURES & CAPITALS

Prefectures	Capitals
Aichi *(aye-chee)*	**Nagoya** *(nah-go-yah)*
Akita *(ah-kee-tah)*	**Akita** *(ah-kee-tah)*
Aomori *(ah-oh-more-ree)*	**Aomori** *(ah-oh-more-ree)*
Chiba *(chee-bah)*	**Chiba** *(chee-bah)*
Ehime *(eh-he-may)*	**Matsuyama** *(mot-sue-yah-mah)*
Fukui *(who-kuu-ee)*	**Fukui** *(who-kuu-ee)*
Fukuoka *(who-kuu-oh-kah)*	**Fukuoka** *(who-kuu-oh-kah)*
Fukushima *(who-kuu-she-mah)*	**Fukushima** *(who-kuu-she-mah)*
Gifu *(ghee-who)*	**Gifu** *(ghee-who)*
Gumma *(gume-mah)*	**Maebashi** *(mah-eh-bah-she)*
Hiroshima *(he-roe-she-mah)*	**Hiroshima** *(he-roe-she-mah)*
Hokkaido *(hoke-kie-doe)*	**Sapporo** *(sop-poe-roe)*
Hyogo *(he-yoe-go)*	**Kobe** *(koh-bay)*
Ibaraki *(ee-bah-rah-kee)*	**Mito** *(me-toe)*
Ishikawa *(e-she-kah-wah)*	**Kanazawa** *(kah-nah-zah-wah)*
Iwate *(ee-wah-tay)*	**Morioka** *(moe-ree-oh-kah)*
Kagawa *(kah-gah-wah)*	**Takamatsu** *(tah-kah-mot-sue)*
Kagoshima *(kah-go-she-mah)*	**Kagoshima** *(kah-go-she-mah)*

Kanagawa
(kah-nah-gah-wah)
Kochi *(koe-chee)*
Kumamoto
(kuu-mah-moe-toe)
Kyoto *(k'yoe-toe)*
Mie *(me-eh)*
Miyagi *(me-yah-ghee)*
Miyazaki *(me-yah-zah-kee)*

Nagano *(nah-gah-no)*
Nagasaki *(nah-gah-sah-kee)*

Nara *(nah-rah)*
Niigata *(nee-gah-tah)*
Oita *(oh-ee-tah)*
Okayama *(oh-kah-yah-mah)*

Okinawa *(oh-kee-nah-wah)*
Osaka *(oh-sah-kah)*
Saga *(sah-gah)*
Saitama *(sie-tah-mah)*
Shiga *(she-gah)*
Shimane *(she-mah-nay)*
Shizuoka *(she-zoo-oh-kah)*

Tochigi *(toe-chee-ghee)*

Tokyo *(toe-k'yoe)*
Tokushima
(toe-kuu-she-mah)
Tottori *(tote-toe-ree)*

Yokohama
(yoe-koe-hah-mah)
Kochi *(koe-chee)*
Kumamoto
(kuu-mah-moe-toe)
Kyoto *(k'yoe-toe)*
Tsu *(t'sue)*
Sendai *(sen-die)*
Miyazaki
(me-yah-zah-kee)
Nagano *(nah-gah-no)*
Nagasaki
(nah-gah-sah-kee)
Nara *(nah-rah)*
Niigata *(nee-gah-tah)*
Oita *(oh-ee-tah)*
Okayama
(oh-kah-yah-mah)
Naha *(nah-hah)*
Osaka *(oh-sah-kah)*
Saga *(sah-gah)*
Saitama *(sie-tah-mah)*
Otsu *(oh-t'sue)*
Matsue *(mo-t'sue-eh)*
Shizuoka
(she-zoo-oh-kah)
Utsunomiya
(uu-t'sue-no-me-yah)
Tokyo *(toe-k'yoe)*
Tokushima
(toe-kuu-she-mah)
Tottori *(tote-toe-ree)*

Toyama *(toe-yah-mah)*
Yamagata
(yah-mah-gah-tah)
Yamaguchi
(yah-mah-guu-chee)
Yamanashi
(yah-mah-nah-she)
Wakayama
(wah-kah-yah-mah)

Toyama *(toe-yah-mah)*
Yamagata
(yah-mah-gah-tah)
Yamaguchi
(yah-mah-guu-chee)
Kofu *(koe-who)*

Wakayama
(wah-kah-yah-mah)

Strictly speaking, Tokyo, Osaka, Kyoto, and Hokkaido are not prefectures. Tokyo is a *to (toe)* と or "metropolis," Kyoto and Osaka are *fu (who)* ふ or "urban areas" and Hokkaido is a *dō (doe)* どう or "district."

IMPORTANT CITY & AREA NAMES

Atami *(ah-tah-me)*
Enoshima *(eh-no-she-mah)*
Fuji-Yoshida *(who-jee-yoe-she-dah)*
Gotenba *(go-tem-bah)*
Hakodate *(hah-koe-dah-tay)*
Hakone *(hah-koe-nay)*
Hamamatsu *(hah-mah-mah-t'sue)*
Himeji *(he-may-jee)*
Ito *(ee-toe)*
Izu *(ee-zoo)*
Kamakura *(kah-mah-kuu-rah)*
Kawasaki *(kah-wah-sah-kee)*
Karuizawa *(kah-rue-ee-zah-wah)*
Kitakyushu *(kee-tah queue-shuu)*

Narita *(nah-ree-tah)*
Nikko *(neek-koe)*
Oshima *(oh-she-mah)*
Takarazuka *(tah-kah-rah-zuu-kah)*
Toba *(toe-bah)*
Yokosuka *(yoe-kose-kah)*
Zushi *(zuu-she)*

NAMES IN TOKYO

Akasaka *(ah-kah-sah-kah)*
Major international hotels, restaurants, bars, nightclubs, and geisha inn district. *Akasaka Mitsuke (ah-kah-sah-kah me-t'sue-kay)* at the west end of the district is a key subway terminal. Hotels here include New Otani Hotel, and Akasaka Excel Hotel Tokyu.
Aoyama *(ah-oh-yah-mah)*
Shops, offices, restaurants, and residential areas.
Asakusa *(ah-sah-kuu-sah)*
Major transportation terminal, entertainment and shopping area.
Akihabara *(ah-kee-hah-bah-rah)*
Noted discount center for electrical appliances and electronic items.
Chiyoda-ku *(chee-yoe-dah kuu)*
Tokyo's main west side "downtown" ward. The Imperial Palace is in this ward.
Chuo-ku *(chuu-oh kuu)*
Tokyo's main east-side "downtown" ward, where the famous Ginza district is located.

Ginza *(geen-zah)*

Tokyo's oldest and probably best known shopping and entertainment district, which now competes with a dozen or so other districts around the city. In the central area of downtown Tokyo.

Hakozaki-cho *(hah-koe-zah-kee-choe)*

This is the location of the Tokyo City Air Terminal (TCAT), which serves both as the main terminal for limousine buses going to and from the New Tokyo International Airport in Narita and as a check-in facility for many international airlines.

Hamamatsu-cho *(hah-mah-mot-sue-choe)*

This is the station in south Tokyo where you board the monorail train for Haneda Airport.

Harajuku *(hah-rah-juu-kuu)*

A booming young people's district on the west side of Tokyo, noted for its fashion boutiques, restaurants, and Sunday afternoon street entertainment. The famous Meiji Shrine is located here.

Hibiya *(he-bee-yah)*

A popular theater and restaurant district adjoining the Imperial Palace grounds on the southeast corner. Also adjoins the Ginza on the east and Shinbashi on the south. A major subway terminal lies beneath its main thoroughfares. The Imperial Hotel is in this area.

Ikebukuro *(ee-kay-buu-kuu-roe)*

An entertainment, shopping, and business center on the northeast side of Tokyo. Several hotels.

Kabuki-cho *(kah-buu-kee-choe)*

The primary entertainment area in Shinjuku Ward, about three blocks north of Shinjuku Station. Filled with theaters, restaurants, cabarets, bars, and "soaplands."

Minato-ku *(me-nah-toe kuu)*

Tokyo's main south side "downtown" ward, where most embassies and many foreign residential areas are located.

Kanda *(kahn-dah)*

An area noted for its bookshops and universities. A key train station is on the east side.

Marunouchi *(mah-rue-no-uu-chee)*

One of Tokyo's main downtown business centers, adjoining the Imperial Palace Grounds on the east side. Banks, trading companies, and Tokyo Station are in this section.

Nihonbashi *(nee-hone-bah-she)*

Tokyo's original financial center (banks, security companies) and shopping center (major department stores and shops of all kinds).

Otemachi *(oh-tay-mah-chee)*

A major financial business and financial center, adjoining the Marunouchi district on the north and the Imperial Palace grounds on the west. A main subway transfer terminal.

Roppongi *(rope-pong-ghee)*

One of Tokyo's most popular restaurant, bar, disco, and night-club areas. On the Hibiya Subway Line and Oedo Subway Line.

Shibuya *(she-buu-yah)*

A major railway/subway terminal, shopping center, theater, and restaurant district. Several businessmen's hotels. Terminus of the Ginza Subway Line.

Shinbashi *(sheem-bah-she)*

Hotels, entertainment, restaurants, and geisha inns. Adjoins the Ginza on the south.

Shinagawa *(she-nah-gah-wah)*

Site of several international hotels, some distance south of the downtown area. Largest collection of hotel rooms in the city.

Shinjuku *(sheen-juu-kuu)*

A main railway terminal, also a noted entertainment and shopping district and the west-side center for office buildings and international hotels.

Toranomon *(toe-rah-no-moan)*

A business and hotel district (Hotel Okura), and the location of the American Embassy.

Ueno *(uu-eh-no)*

A main railway and subway terminal, also noted for Ueno Park and its middle-class restaurants, shops, and businessmen's hotels.

Yaesu-guchi *(yah-eh-sue guu-chi)*

East side of Tokyo Station, where the "bullet train" platforms are located. In Japanese, these trains are known as ***shinkansen** (sheen-kahn-sen)* しんかんせん or "new trunk lines." If you are going to board the trains and are going to the station by taxi, tell the driver to take you to the Yaesu-guchi side of Tokyo Station.

Yotsuya *(yoe-t'sue-yah)*

Location of Sophia University or Jochi Daigaku; good site for viewing cherry blossoms in April.

Yurakucho *(yuu-rah-kuu-choe)*

Heart of what is usually considered the downtown area of Tokyo, surrounded by the Marunouchi business district, the Ginza entertainment/shopping area, and the Hibiya entertainment and Imperial Hotel district. The station is two short blocks from the southeast corner of the Imperial Palace Grounds.

NAMES IN KYOTO

Fushimi-ku *(who-she-me kuu)* Fushimi Ward
Higashiyama-ku *(he-gah-she-yah-mah kuu)*
  Higashiyama Ward
Kamigyo-ku *(kah-me-g'yoe kuu)* Kamigyo Ward
Kita-ku *(kee-tah kuu)* Kita Ward
Minami-ku *(me-nah-me kuu)* Minami Ward
Nakagyo-ku *(nah-kah-g'yoe kuu)* Nakagyo Ward
Sakyo-ku *(sah-k'yoe kuu)* Sakyo Ward
Shimogyo-ku *(she-moe-g'yoe kuu)* Shimogyo Ward
Ukyo-ku *(uu-k'yoe kuu)* Ukyo Ward

Arashiyama *(ah-rah-she-yah-mah)* a historical spot in the
  northwestern area of Kyoto
Fushimi *(who-she-me)* the famous Fushimi Inari-taisha
  Shrine is located in this area
Gion-machi *(ghee-own mah-chee)* Kyoto's famed Geisha
  district
Higashiyama *(he-gah-she-yah-mah)* major sightseeing
  spots are concentrated in this area
Kurama *(kue-rah-mah)* the famous Kurama-dera Temple
  and Kifune Shrine are located in this area
Nishijin *(nee-she-jeen)* an area famous for silk-weaving

Gojo-dori *(go-joe doe-ree)* a major street
Hachijo-dori *(hah-chee-joe doe-ree)*
  a major thoroughfare
Higashiyama-dori *(he-gah-she-yah-mah doe-ree)*
  a major thoroughfare
Karasuma-dori *(kah-rah-sue-mah doe-ree)*
  a major business district

Kawaramachi-dori *(kah-wah-rah-muh-chee doe-ree)*
a popular shopping street
Oike-dori *(oh-ee-kay doe-ree)*
a main street near Nijo castle
Omiya-dori *(oh-me-hah doe-ree)* "Temple Street"
Shijo-dori *(she-joe doe-ree)* a main street

Aoi-matsuri *(ah-oh-ee mot-sue-ree)* a major festival
Daitoku-ji *(die-toe-kuu jee)* a famous temple
Ginkaku-ji *(gheen-kah-kuu jee)* the Silver Pavilion
Gion-matsuri *(ghee-own mot-sue-ree)* a major festival
Heian-jingu *(hay-ahn-jeen-guu)* Heian Shrine
Jidai-matsuri *(jee-die mot-sue-ree)* a major festival
Kaburenjo *(kah-buu-rane-joe)* a famous theater
Katsura Rikyu *(kot-sue-rah ree-queue)* the famed Katsura
Imperial Villa
Kinkaku-ji *(keen-kah-kuu jee)*
the famous Temple of the Golden Pavilion
Kiyomizu-dera *(kee-yoe-me-zuu day-rah)*
one of Kyoto's most spectacular temples
Kyoto Gosho *(k'yoe-toe go-show)*
Kyoto Imperial Palace
Nanzen-ji *(nahn-zen-jee)* a famous temple
Nijo-jo *(nee-joe-joe)*
Nijo Castle, probably Kyoto's most famous castle-palace
Sanjusangendo *(sahn-juu-sahn-gane-doe)*
a famous temple
Shinsen-en *(sheen-sen-en)* a famous Japanese-style garden
Shokoku-ji *(show-koe-kuu-jee)* a renowned temple
Shugakuin Rikyu *(shuu-gah-kuu-een ree-queue)*
Imperial Villa

NAMES IN OSAKA

Abenobashi *(ah-bay-no-bah-she)* shopping area
Dotonbori *(doe-tome-boe-ree)* entertainment district
Honmachi *(hone-mah-chee)* business district
Minami *(me-nah-me)* a famous entertainment district
Nakanoshima *(nah-kah-no-she-mah)* civic center, on a
  small island
Nanba *(Nahm-bah)* shopping center, including huge
  underground malls
Nanba Walk *(Nahm-bah uu-oh-kuu)* underground shopping
  center, between Nanba station and Nipponbashi station
Sakuranomiya *(sah-kuu-rah-no-me-yah)* a park
Shinsaibashi *(sheen-sie-bah-she)* shopping area
Shinsekai *(sheen say-kie)* "New World" amusement center
Umeda *(uu-may-dah)* shopping center / business district
Yodoyabashi *(yoe-doh-yah-bah-she)* business district
Ebisubashi-suji *(eh-bee-sue-bah-she sue-jee)*
  main thoroughfare
Mido-suji *(me-doe sue-jee)* main thoroughfare
Shinsaibashi-suji *(sheen-sie-bah-she sue-jee)*
  main thoroughfare

DEPARTMENT STORES

Daimaru *(die-mah-rue)*
Fujii-Daimaru *(who-jee-ee die-mah-rue)*
Hankyu *(hahn-queue)*
Hanshin *(hahn-sheen)*
Isetan *(ee-say-tahn)*
Keio *(kay-ee-oh)*

Kintetsu *(keen-tay-t'sue)*
Matsuya *(mot-sue-yah)*
Matsuzakaya *(mot-sue-zah-kah-yah)*
Mitsukoshi *(meet-sue-koe-she)*
Odakyu *(oh-dah-queue)*
Printemps *(puu-ran-tahn)*
Seibu *(say-ee-buu)*
Takashimaya *(tah-kah-she-mah-yah)*
Tobu *(toe-buu)*
Tokyu *(toe-queue)*

MAJOR NEWSPAPERS

Asahi Shinbun *(ah-sa-hee sheem-boon)*
Chunichi Shinbun *(chuu-nee-chee sheem-boon)*
Hokkaido Shinbun *(hoek-kie-doh sheem-boon)*
Mainichi Shinbun *(my-nee-chee sheem-boon)*
Nihon Keizai Shinbun
  (nee-hoan kay-ee-zie sheem-boon)
Nikkan Kogyo Shinbun
  (neek-kahn koag-yoe sheem boon)
Nikkan Sports *(neek-kahn spoe-t'sue)*
Nishi-nihon Shinbun
  (nee-shee nee-hoan sheem-boon)
Sankei Shinbun *(sahn-kay-ee sheem-boon)*
Tokyo Shinbun *(toe-k'yoe sheem-boon)*
Yomiuri Shinbun *(yoe-me-uu-ree sheem-boon)*

Leading English language newspapers in Tokyo:
The Japan Times, The Japan News

MAJOR INDUSTRIAL ZONES

Chukyo *(chuu-k'yoe)* Aichi and Mie Prefectures
Hanshin *(hahn-sheen)* Osaka and Hyogo Prefectures
Hokuriku *(hoe-kuu-ree-kuu)* Niigata, Toyama, Fukui, and Ishikawa Prefectures
Keihin *(kay-ee-heen)* Tokyo and Kanagawa Prefectures
Keiyo *(kay-ee-yoe)* Tokyo and Chiba Prefectures
Kitakyushu *(kee-tah queue-shuu)* Fukuoka Prefecture
Setouchi *(say-toe-uu-chee)* Okayama, Hiroshima, Kagawa, and Ehime Prefectures
Tokai *(toe-kie)* Aichi, Gifu, Mie, and Shizuoka Prefectures

OTHER COMMON TERMS

aka-chochin *(ah-kah choe-cheen)*—Large, red paper lanterns used by drinking and traditionally styled eating places as symbols of their trade.

gaijin *(guy-jeen)*—This literally means "outside person" and is the common but slightly derogatory Japanese term for "foreigner." **Gaikoku-jin** *(guy-koe-kuu-jeen)* or more polite **gaikoku-no-kata** *(guy-koe-kuu-no-kah-tah)* "foreign person" is preferred in formal situations.

jan-ken-pon *(jahn-ken-pone)*—The "paper/scissors/stone" hand-game, played on a variety of occasions, for fun as well as for points of order. Also, **jan-ken** *(jahn-ken)*.

jishin *(jee-shen)*—An "earthquake." The Great East Japan Earthquake *Higashi Nihon Daishinsai* *(he-gah-she nee-hoan die-sheen-sie)* happened on March 11, 2011.

kapusel hoteru *(kah-poo-sell hoe-tay-rue)*—Capsule hotels, a type of accommodation facility with very small capsule-like rooms. It is a unique hotel concept from Japan, and such hotels are booming now.

kawa / gawa *(kah-wah / gah-wah)* "River."

kazan *(kah-sahn)* a "volcano." The volcanic nature of the terrain in Japan means that there are over 2,000 hotsprings *onsen (own-sen)* across the country.

koban *(koe-bahn)*—The police box system. **Koban** are staffed with police officers 24 hours a day, for example, the **Koban** located in the most popular tourist areas, Ginza, Asakusa, Shibuya or Shinjuku.

kogen *(koe-gain)*—This word is often seen as part of a place-name, particularly those having to do with recreational resorts. It means "heights" and refers to a location in the high-lands.

matsuri *(mot-sue-ree)*—Another word that is frequently used without translation, it means "festival," of which there are thousands in Japan each year, ranging from tiny neighbor-hood-shrine celebrations to major national events.

nagata-cho *(nah-gah-tah-choe)*—This is the section in Tokyo where the Diet building and other key government buildings along with the prime minister's official residence are located. It is often used in the sense of "the government."

noren *(no-rane)*—These are the short, split indigo blue cur-tains that are hung over the entrances to Japanese-style eating and drinking places. Shops that serve sushi, noodles, tempura, and the like generally use **noren** (*no-rane*). The **noren** (*no-rane*) are normally hung up when the place opens for business, and taken down when it closes. **Noren** (*no-rane*) and their emblems have traditionally served as the banner/logo of restaurants and other places of business with long histories.

shinkansen (*sheen-kahn-sen*)—These are the highspeed express trains that foreigners commonly refer to as the "bullet trains." The words mean "new trunk lines."

te-miyage (*tay-me-yah-gay*) and **o-miyage** (*oh-me-yah-gay*) —These are the "hand gifts" that Japanese carry when on trips, especially trips abroad, to give to people whom they meet for business or who befriend them. In some business situations, the gifts may be very expensive, but generally they are small tokens.

tsunami (*t'se-nah-mee*)—a seismic sea wave "Tsunami." If a big earthquake happened, you should take refuge on high grounds.

washlet (*uu-oh-shuu-let*)—a bidet toilet seats. In Japan, bidet toilet seats are commonly found at sightseeing attractions, hotels, department stores, airports and so on.

zashiki (*zah-she-kee*)—Translated rather freely, this means a room or rooms in which the floor is made of **tatami** (*tah-tah-me*) たたみ or reed-mats, the traditional Japanese style of flooring where one sits on the floor. Restaurants serving traditional Japanese-style food often have rooms with **tatami** (*tah-tah-me*) たたみ mat floors, and ask patrons if they want a **zashiki** (*zah-she-kee*) ざしき or a Western style room.

PART THREE
General Word List

[A]

address	*jūsho (juu-show)*	じゅうしょ
age	*toshi (toe-she)*	とし
air-conditioning	*eakon (ayj-ah kone)*	エアコン
airmail	*kōkū-bin (koe-kuu-bean)*	こうくうびん
airplane	*hikōki (he-koe-kee)*	ひこうき
airport	*kūkō (kuu-koe)*	くうこう
April	*shigatsu (she-got-sue)*	しがつ
arrive	*tsukimasu (t'sue-kee-mahss)*	つきます
August	*hachigatsu (hah-chee-got-sue)*	はちがつ
automobile	*jidōsha (jee-doe-shah)*	じどうしゃ

[B]

bank	*ginkō (geen-koe)*	ぎんこう
bar	*bā (bah)*	バー
bath	*o-furo (oh-fuu-roe)*	おふろ
beautiful	*utsukushii (oo-t'sue-koo-shee)*	うつくしい
beef	*bīfu (bee-who)*	ビーフ
birthday	*tanjōbi (tahn-joe-bee)*	たんじょうび
book	*hon (hone)*	ほん
bookstore	*hon'ya (hone-yah)*	ほんや
box lunch (Japanese-style)	*bentō (oh-ben-toe)*	べんとう
bread	*pan (pahn)*	パン
breakfast	*asagohan (ah-sah-go-hahn)*	あさごはん
bridge	*hashi (hah-she)*	はし
building	*biru (be-rue)*	ビル
bus	*basu (bah-sue)*	バス

[C]

cabaret	*kyabarē (k'yah-bah-ray)*	キャバレー
camera	*kamera (kah-may-rah)*	カメラ
car	*kuruma (koo-rue-mah)*	くるま
chair	*isu (ee-sue)*	いす
change (money returned)	*o-tsuri (oh-t'sue-ree)*	おつり
change (small coins)	*kozeni (koe-zay-nee)*	こぜに
children	*kodomo (koe-doe-moe)*	こども
chopsticks	*o-hashi (oh-hah-she)*	おはし
cold (illness)	*kaze (kah-zay)*	かぜ
catch a cold	*kaze-o hikimasu (kah-zay oh he-kee-mahss)*	かぜを ひきます
congratulations	*omedetō gozaimasu (oh-may-day-toe go-zie-mahss)*	おめでとう ございます
corner	*kado (kah-doe)*	かど
cover charge	*kabā chāji (kah-bah-chah-jee)*	カバー チャージ

[D]

date (time of the month)	*hizuke (he-zoo-kay)*	ひづけ
daughter	*musume (moo-sue-may)*	むすめ
daytime	*hiruma (he-rue-mah)*	ひるま
day after tomorrow	*asatte (ah-saht-tay)*	あさって
December	*jū-ni-gatsu (juu-nee-got-sue)*	じゅうにがつ
deliver	*todokemasu (toe-doe-kay-mahss)*	とどけます
dentist	*ha-isha (hai-shah)*	はいしゃ
departure	*shuppatsu (shupe-pot-sue)*	しゅっぱつ
deposit (for room)	*tetsukekin (tay-tsue-kay-keen)*	てつけきん
dessert	*dezāto (day-zah-toe)*	デザート

dining car	*shokudōsha*	しょくどうしゃ
	(show-koo-doe shah)	
dining room	*shokudō* (show-kuu-doe)	しょくどう
dinner, evening meal	*yūshoku* (yuu-show-kuu)	ゆうしょく
drink	*nomimono* (no-me-moe-no)	のみもの
discount	*waribiki* (wah-ree-bee-kee)	わりびき
dollar	*doru* (doe-rue)	ドル
double room	*daburu (rūmu)*	ダブル(ルーム)
	(dah-boo-rue (rue-moo))	
driver	*untenshu* (oon-ten-shoo)	うんてんしゅ
drugstore	*yakkyoku* (yahk-k'yoe-koo)	やっきょく
drycleaning	*dorai kurīningu*	ドライクリーニング
	(doe-rye koo-ree-neen-goo)	

[E]

east	*higashi* (he-gah-she)	ひがし
eel	*unagi* (oo-nah-ghee)	うなぎ
embassy	*taishikan* (tai-she-kahn)	たいしかん
egg	*tamago* (tah-mah-go)	たまご
England	*Igirisu* (ee-ghee-ree-sue)	イギリス
entrance	*iriguchi* (ee-ree-goo-chee)	いりぐち
evening	*yūgata* (yuu-gah-tah)	ゆうがた
this evening	*konban* (kome-bahn)	こんばん
exit	*deguchi* (day-goo-chee)	でぐち
express train	*kyūkō* (cue-koe)	きゅうこう
expressway, motorway	*kōsokudōro*	こうそくどうろ
	(koe-soe-koo-doe-roe)	
eye	*me* (may)	め
glasses, spectacles	*megane* (may-gah-nay)	めがね

[F]

fall, autumn	*aki* (ah-kee)	あき
February	*ni-gatsu* (nee-got-sue)	にがつ
fee	*tesūryō* (tay-sue-r'yoe)	てすうりょう

festival	*o-matsuri (oh-maht-sue-ree)*	おまつり
fever	*netsu (neh-t'sue)*	ねつ
first-class (tickets)	*fāsuto kurasu (fai-sue-toe koo-rah-sue)*	ファースト クラス
fish	*sakana (sah-kah-nah)*	さかな
foreign	*gaikoku-no (guy-koe-koo)*	がいこくの
foreigner	*gaikokujin (guy-koe-koo-jeen)*	がいこくじん
France	*Furansu (fuu-rahn-sue)*	フランス
front desk, reception desk	*furonto (fuu-roan-toe)*	フロント
fruit	*kudamono (koo-dah-moe-no)*	くだもの

[G]

gallery	*gyararī (g'yah-rah-ree)*	ギャラリー
garden	*niwa (nee-wah)*	にわ
garlic	*ninniku (neen-nee-koo)*	にんにく
genuine	*honmono-no (home-moe-no no)*	ほんものの
Germany	*Doitsu (doe-ee-t'sue)*	ドイツ
get off (disembark)	*orimasu (oh-ree-mahss)*	おります
get on, embark	*norimasu (no-ree-mahss)*	のります
glasses (spectacles)	*megane (may-gah-nay)*	めがね
gram	*guramu (goo-rah-moo)*	グラム
guest	*o-kyakusan / o-kyakusama (oh-k'yah-koo sahn) / (oh-k'yah-koo sah-mah)*	おきゃくさん おきゃくさま

[H]

hand	*te (tay)*	て
hanger (for clothing)	*hangā (hahn-gah)*	ハンガー
heart attack	*shinzō-mahi (sheen-zoe mah-hee)*	しんぞうまひ

heavy	*omoi* (owe-moy)	おもい
holiday	*kyūjitsu* (cue-jee-t'sue)	きゅうじつ
home	*uchi* (oo-chee)	うち
horseradish	*wasabi* (wah-sah-bee)	わさび
hospital	*byōin* (b'yoeh-een)	びょういん
hot (spicy)	*karai* (kah-rye)	からい
hot spring	*onsen* (own-sen)	おんせん
house (structure)	*ie* (ee-eh)	いえ
hungry	*onaka-ga sukimasu* (oh-nah-kah gah ski-mass)	おなかが すきます
hurry	*isogimasu* (ee-so-ghee-mass)	いそぎます
painful, sore	*itai* (ee-tai)	いたい

[I]

inn (Japanese style)	*ryokan* (r'yoe-kahn)	りょかん
international	*kokusai* (coke-sai)	こくさい
international telephone (call)	*kokusai denwa* (koke-sai den-wah)	こくさいでんわ
intersection, crossroads	*kōsaten* (koe-sah-ten)	こうさてん
introduce	*shōkai suru* (show-kie sue-rue)	しょうかいする
introduction (written)	*shōkaijō* (show-kie-joe)	しょうかいじょう

[J]

January	*ichi-gatsu* (ee-chee-got-sue)	いちがつ
Japan	*Nihon* (nee-hone)	にほん
Japanese-style bed	*futon* (fuu-tone)	ふとん
Japanese-style room	*Nihon-ma* (nee-hone-mah)	にほんま
job	*shigoto* (she-go-toe)	しごと
July	*shichi-gatsu* (she-chee-got-sue)	しちがつ

| June | *roku-gatsu (roe-koo-got-sue)* | ろくがつ |

[K]

key	*kagi (kah-ghee)*	かぎ
kilogram	*kiro (kee-roe)*	キロ
kilometer	*kiro (kee-roe)*	キロ
kind (nice)	*shinsetsu (shin-set-sue)*	しんせつ
Korea (South)	*Kankoku (kahn-koe-koo)*	かんこく
Korean (language)	*Kankokugo (kahn-koe-koo-go)*	かんこくご
Korean (person)	*Kankoku-jin (kahn-koe-koo-jeen)*	かんこくじん

[L]

last (final)	*saigo (sai-go)*	さいご
last day	*saigo-no hi (sai-go no hee)*	さいごの ひ
last month	*sengetsu (sen-get-sue)*	せんげつ
last week	*senshū (sen shuu)*	せんしゅう
last year	*kyonen (k'yoe-nen)*	きょねん
laundry	*sentakumono (sen-tah-koo-moe-no)*	せんたくもの
left (direction/side)	*hidari (he-dah-ree)*	ひだり
letter	*tegami (teh-gah-me)*	てがみ
luggage	*nimotsu (nee-moat-sue)*	にもつ
lunch	*hirugohan (he-rue-go-hahn)*	ひるごはん

[M]

maid	*meido (may-e-doe)*	メイド
man (male)	*otoko (oh-toe-koe)*	おとこ
manager	*manējā (mah-nay-jah)*	マネージャー
map	*chizu (chee-zoo)*	ちず
March	*san-gatsu (sahn-got-sue)*	さんがつ
May	*go-gatsu (go-got-sue)*	ごがつ
meal ticket	*shokken (shoke-ken)*	しょっけん
meat	*niku (nee-koo)*	にく

medicine	*kusuri (koo-sue-ree)*	くすり
menu	*menyū (men-yuu)*	メニュー
morning	*asa (ah-sah)*	あさ
movie	*eiga (a-e-gah)*	えいが

[N]

name card	*meishi (may-she)*	めいし
napkin	*napukin (nahp-keen)*	ナプキン
New Year's	*o-shō-gatsu (oh-show-got-sue)*	おしょうがつ
next	*tsugi (t'sue-ghee)*	つぎ
next month	*raigetsu (rye-get-sue)*	らいげつ
next week	*raishū (rye-shuu)*	らいしゅう
next year	*rainen (rye-nane)*	らいねん
night	*yoru (yoe-rue)*	よる
nightclub	*naito kurabu (nai-toe koo-rah-boo)*	ナイト クラブ
north	*kita (kee-tah)*	きた
November	*jū-ichi-gatsu (juu-ee-chee-got-sue)*	じゅういちがつ

[O]

October	*jū-gatsu (juu-got-sue)*	じゅうがつ
once	*ichido (ee-chee-doe)*	いちど
one-way (street)	*ippō tsūkō (eep-poe t'sue-koe)*	いっぽうつうこう
one-way (ticket)	*kata-michi (kah-tah-mee-chee)*	かたみち
onion	*tamanegi (tah-mah-nay-ghee)*	たまねぎ

[P]

package, parcel	*kozutsumi (koe-zoot-sue-me)*	こづつみ
paper	*kami (kah-me)*	かみ
park, recreational area	*kōen (koe-en)*	こうえん
parking	*chūshajō (choo-shah-joe)*	ちゅうしゃじょう

passport	*pasupōto (pah-sue-poe-toe)*	パスポート
pearls	*shinju (sheen-juu)*	しんじゅ
pepper	*koshō (koe-show)*	こしょう
platform (train)	*hōmu (hoe-moo)*	ホーム
police box (small sub-station on street)	*kōban (koe-bahn)*	こうばん
policeman	*o-mawari-san (oh-mah-wah-ree-sahn)*	おまわりさん
post office	*yūbinkyoku (yuu-bean k'yoe-kuu)*	ゆうびんきょく
potato	*jagaimo (jah-guy-ee-moe)*	じゃがいも
pottery	*tōki (toe-kee)*	とうき

[R]

refrigerator	*reizōko (ray-e-zoe-koe)*	れいぞうこ
refund	*harai-modoshi (hah-rye-moe-doe-she)*	はらいもどし
rent (n)	*yachin (yah-cheen)*	やちん
repair	*naoshimasu (nah-oh-she-mahss)*	なおします
reservation	*yoyaku (yoe-yah-koo)*	よやく
reserved seat	*shiteiseki (ssh-tay-seh-kee)*	していせき
restaurant (Japanese)	*ryōriya (rio-ree-yah)*	りょうりや
restaurant (Western)	*resutoran (res-toe-ran)*	レストラン
rice (cooked white rice)	*gohan (go-hahn)*	ごはん
right (direction/side)	*migi (mee-ghee)*	みぎ
road	*michi (mee-chee)*	みち
room	*heya (hay-yah)*	へや
room (Japanese-style)	*nihon-ma (nee-hone-mah)*	にほんま
room (Western-style)	*yō-ma (yoe-mah)*	ようま

room number	*rūmu nambā* *(rue-moo nahm-bah)*	ルーム ナンバー
room service	*rūmu sābisu* *(rue-moo sah-bee-sue)*	ルーム サービス

[S]

salt	*shio (she-oh)*	しお
schedule (plan)	*yotei (yoe-tay)*	よてい
school	*gakkō (gahk-koe)*	がっこう
sea (ocean)	*umi (oo-me)*	うみ
seamail	*funabin (fuu-nah-bean)*	ふなびん
seasick	*funayoi (fuu-nah-yoe-e)*	ふなよい
seaside	*kaigan (kai-gahn)*	かいがん
season	*kisetsu (kee-set-sue)*	きせつ
seat	*seki (seh-kee)*	せき
seat number	*zaseki bangō* *(zah-say-kee bahn-go)*	ざせき ばんごう
September	*ku-gatsu (koo-got-sue)*	くがつ
service center	*sābisu sentā* *(sah-bee-sue sen-tah)*	サービス センター
ship	*fune (fuu-nay)*	ふね
shirt	*shatsu (shah-t'sue)*	シャツ
shrine	*jinja (jeen-jah)*	じんじゃ
single room	*shinguru (sheen-goo-rue)*	シングル
slow	*yukkuri (yuke-koo-ree)*	ゆっくり
soap	*sekken (sek-ken)*	せっけん
son	*musuko (moo-sue-koe)*	むすこ
south	*minami (me-nah-me)*	みなみ
souvenir (gift)	*omiyage (oh-me-yah-gay)*	おみやげ
soy sauce	*shōyu (show-yuu)*	しょうゆ
spicy	*karai (kah-rye)*	からい
spoon	*supūn (su-poon)*	スプーン
spring	*haru (hah-rue)*	はる
stamp (for mail)	*kitte (keet-tay)*	きって
stop (bus/train)	*teiryūjo (tay-e-r'yoo-joe)*	ていりゅうじょ

straight (direction)	*massugu (mahss-sue-goo)*	まっすぐ
sugar	*satō (sah-toe)*	さとう
summer	*natsu (not-sue)*	なつ
supermarket	*sūpā (sue-pah)*	スーパー

[T]

table	*tēburu (tay-boo-rue)*	テーブル
tag (label)	*harigami (hah-ree-gah-me)*	はりがみ
taxi stand	*takushī noriba (tock-she no-ree-bah)*	タクシー のりば
tea (black/brown)	*kōcha (koe-chah)*	こうちゃ
tea (Japanese green tea)	*nihon-cha (nee-hone-chah)*	にほんちゃ
television	*terebi (tay-ray-bee)*	テレビ
temperature (body)	*taion (tai-own)*	たいおん
temperature (weather)	*ondo (own-doe)*	おんど
temple	*o-tera (oh-tay-rah)*	おてら
theater (movies)	*eigakan (a-e-gah-kahn)*	えいがかん
ticket	*kippu (keep-poo)*	きっぷ
ticket window (vending machines)	*kippu uriba (keep-poo oo-ree-bah)*	きっぷ うりば
today	*kyō (k'yoe)*	きう
toilet	*o-tearai (oh-tay-ah-rye)*	おてあらい
tonight	*konban (kome-bahn)*	こんばん
traffic	*kōtsū (kote-sue)*	こうつう
traffic light	*shingō (sheen-go)*	しんごう
traveler's checks	*toraberāzu chekku (toe-rah-bay-rah-zoo check-ku)*	トラベラーズ チェック
twin room (two persons, two beds)	*tsuin (t'sue-ween)*	ツイン

[V]

vegetables	*yasai (yah-sai)*	やさい
video	*bideotēpu (beedeo-taapuu)*	ビデオテープ
visa	*biza (bee-zah)*	ビザ
visiting card	*meishi (may-e-she)*	めいし

[W]

waiter	*uētā (way-tah)*	ウエーター
wallet	*saifu (sai-fuu)*	さいふ
washroom	*o-tearai (oh-tay-ah-rye)*	おてあらい
watch (timepiece)	*tokei (to-kay)*	とけい
way (direction)	*michi (me-chee)*	みち
weather	*tenki (ten-kee)*	てんき
weather forecast	*tenki yohō (ten-kee yoe-hoe)*	てんきよほう
west	*nishi (nee-she)*	にし
window	*mado (mah-doe)*	まど
winter	*fuyu (fuu-yoo)*	ふゆ
woman	*onna-no hito (own-nah no ssh-toe)*	おんなの ひと
wonderful	*subarashii (sue-bah-rah-she)*	すばらしい

[Y]

yesterday	*kinō (kee-no-oh)*	きのう
young	*wakai (wah-kai)*	わかい
youth hostel	*yūsu hosuteru (yoo-sue hos-tay-rue)*	ユースホステル

[Z]

zoo	*dōbutsuen (doe-boot-sue-en)*	どうぶつえん